THE
STORY
YOU TELL
YOURSELF

- Or -

How to Read Yourself Like a Book

ALSO BY ROBERT T. YARBOROUGH

Beyond Space and Time

Getting Down to Brass Tacks

The Outrage Paradox

Be Done With It

Quantum Whispers

The New Science of Getting Rich

THE STORY YOU TELL YOURSELF

How to Change Your Inner Narrative

- Or -

How to Read Yourself Like a Book
and Unlock the Secrets to
Understanding Your True Self

Robert T. Yarborough

Pranava Books

Publisher's Cataloging-in-Publication Data
Yarborough, Robert T., 1960–
The Story You Tell Yourself: How to Change Your Inner Narrative; or, How to Read Yourself Like a Book / by Robert T. Yarborough.
— First edition.
p. cm.
Includes bibliographical references.

ISBN: 979-8-9912582-9-6
    1. Self-talk. 2. Identity (Psychology). 3. Personal transformation. 4. Mindfulness. 5. Self-actualization (Psychology). I. Title.
    BF697.5.S43 Y37 2025
    158 — dc23
LCCN: 2025906032

Printed in the United States of America
10 9 8 7 6 5 4 3 2 1

In Memory

———

Robert "Bobby" Claude Yarborough (1930 – 2003)
and Barbara Ella Davis Yarborough (1935 – 2008)

My incredible parents—

Thank you for giving me the freedom to write my own story, even when I was still entangled in the ones I hadn't yet questioned.

Your quiet trust, even in absence, continues to guide my pages.

Dedication

———

Sparrow, Sydney, and Sage.

Always know that you are not the stories others give you. Trust the quiet voice inside you; it is not your enemy. You are never bound by the past.

You are the one who chooses what comes next in you story.

With all my love,

Dad

Table of Contents

PART TWO
Reading Between the Lines

PART THREE
Editing and Rewriting Your Story

Author's Preface

____

"At the center of your being, you have the answer; you know who you are and you know what you want."

— Lao Tzu

I am not a therapist, philosopher, or guru. I do not present myself as someone with ultimate answers or final truths. Like you, I am a human being—imperfect, learning, remembering, forgetting, and starting again.

This book was not written from a place of arrival, but from a place of returning. Again and again. Returning to the self beneath the performance. The awareness beneath the thought. The truth beneath the story.

I've spent many years living inside narratives that were never really mine. Narratives about who I was supposed to be, how I was meant to show up, what it meant to succeed, or to belong. Some were inherited. Some were self-imposed. Most were unconscious.

But beneath those stories, there was always something else— something still, watchful, and quietly waiting to be read.

This book is not a roadmap. It is a mirror. It does not offer steps to becoming someone new, but invitations to see more clearly the person you've always been—before the roles, before the masks, before the conditioning.

If there is wisdom here, it was not born from knowing, but from noticing. From witnessing my own mind in motion—how it sought approval, resisted change, clung to identity, feared vulnerability. And from discovering, in brief and beautiful moments, that I was not the noise but the awareness of it.

Those are the moments this book is made of.

This Book Exists Because I Needed it.

I needed to be reminded that my story is not fixed. That identity can be rewritten. That the inner dialogue shaping my reality is not truth, but habit. I needed to remember that the voice in my head is not who I am—and that I have the power to step out of old narratives and into presence, again and again.

I wrote this book because I've wrestled with self-doubt. Because I've hesitated at the edge of change. Because I've spent years trying to become acceptable to others, only to realize that wholeness was never out there to be earned.

If these words resonate with you, it is not because they are profound—it is because they are shared. This is not one person's story.

This is all of ours.

Reading Yourself Like a Book

To "read yourself like a book" is not to dissect or analyze, but to witness gently. To turn the pages of your own experience with presence rather than judgment. It means becoming curious about the thoughts you've believed, the roles you've played, and the identities you've clung to—and asking, *Are these still true?*

It means seeing the inner dialogue not as who you are, but as something you are listening to. And realizing that if you can hear the voice, you are not the voice. You are the listener.

This book invites you to return to that place of listening.

An Invitation

As you move through these pages, I invite you not to rush. Let the space between the words speak to you. Let the questions stay open. Let the insights rise slowly, not as answers to memorize, but as truths to remember.

Take what resonates. Leave what doesn't. And trust your own inner knowing to guide you through.

You are not alone in this journey. You are not broken. You are not late. You are not behind. You are unfolding. Moment by moment. Page by page.

There is nothing more powerful than the moment you stop living a borrowed story and begin living the one that is truly yours.

Thank you for allowing me to walk beside you as you read yourself like a book.

May you find, in these pages, not a prescription for who to become—but the peace of finally meeting who you are.

With gratitude…

—Robert T. Yarborough
March 2025

Introduction

"Until you make the unconscious conscious, it will direct your life and you will call it fate."

— Carl Jung

There is a moment—quiet, subtle—when you realize the story you've been living is not the only one available.

Not the one written for you.

Not the one shaped by fear.

But something softer. Truer. Still unwritten.

From childhood, you were handed lines to speak, roles to play, labels to wear. You memorized them so well you forgot they weren't yours. You adapted. You performed. You became legible to the world—but unreadable to yourself.

This book is not about fixing what is broken. It's about seeing what was never broken to begin with.

It will not tell you who to be.

It will remind you how to listen.

How to become still enough to notice the patterns, the loops, the voices that are not your own.

In these pages, you won't be asked to become someone new. You'll be invited to become honest. Present. Uncovered. Each chapter is a mirror. Each question, a doorway.

You will be asked to observe—not judge.

To respond—not react.

To read yourself—not as a character in someone else's narrative, but as the author of your own becoming.

There will be resistance. That's part of the reading. There will be voices of doubt. That's part of the editing. But beneath them, there is something that does not shift.

Stillness.

Clarity.

Presence.

This is where your story begins—not in the world's version of who you are, but in the moment you stop pretending and start paying attention.

When you explore the story you tell yourself, you don't find all the answers.

You find something better:

The space to ask the right questions.

And from there, the next page is yours to write.

PART ONE

Understanding the Chapters of Your Life

"We are not the stories we tell ourselves, but the stories we choose to believe."

— Brené Brown

Every great book has a beginning, a middle, and a transformation. But before you can change your story, you have to understand what has been written so far. This section will guide you through the first steps of self-reading—exploring your past influences, key life events, and the roles you've played.

By recognizing the themes and characters in your life so far, you'll gain clarity on the patterns shaping your story—and whether they still serve you

Chapter One

The Concept of Self-Reading

"Until you make the unconscious conscious, it will direct your life, and you will call it fate."
— Carl Jung

There is a stillness beneath the movement of your life. A presence that observes without judgment, without attachment. It watches the unfolding of events, the formation of beliefs, and the repetition of patterns. It is not bound by past or future. It simply is.

To read yourself like a book is to awaken to this presence. It is to step out of the stream of thought and see—clearly, without distortion—the unfolding narrative of your life.

Like a book, your life is composed of chapters, transitions, turning points, and underlying themes. Yet, who is writing it?

Are you merely a character lost in the story, reacting to twists and turns? Or are you the one observing, choosing, and realizing that the story is not who you are?

To become conscious of your own story is the beginning of transformation. But not transformation in the way the mind understands it—some grand effort toward self-improvement, another layer of identity to build upon. No, true transformation is something far simpler: *awareness*.

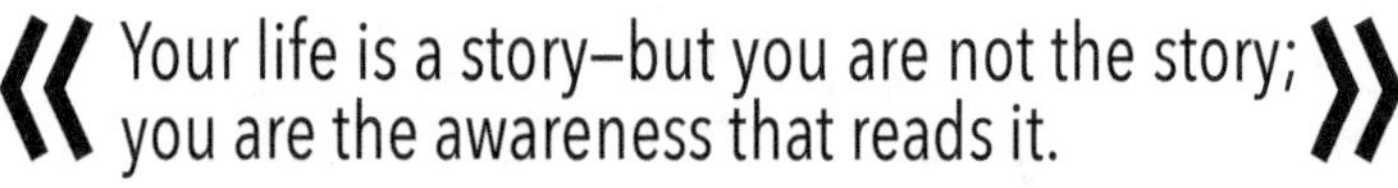

Self-reading means seeing what has always been there yet was hidden beneath the noise of thought.

In practical terms, it involves:

» **Identifying Your Chapters** – Recognizing the events, transitions, and relationships that have shaped your sense of self.

» **Understanding Your Narrative** – Becoming aware of the story your mind tells about who you are.

» **Recognizing Recurring Themes** – Observing the thought patterns, emotional responses, and habitual behaviors that define your experience.

» **Editing and Rewriting** – Questioning what no longer serves you and dissolving the limitations of the past.

If you do not see the story you are living, it will continue, cycling endlessly, as if the pages of a book turn without a reader. But the moment awareness arises, the moment you see, you step outside the script. You realize:

You are not the ink on the page. You are the *space* in which the story unfolds.

Why Self-Awareness is the Foundation of Personal Transformation

To be lost in the story is to be asleep. To awaken is to recognize that you are both the reader and the author.

A book cannot change its words, but the awareness that reads it can shift its meaning. Your life story is not fixed; it is shaped by the lens through which you perceive it. Most people remain unaware of this, believing themselves trapped by their past, defined by the thoughts and emotions that arise within them. But when you bring presence to your experience, you begin to see that the narrative of your mind does not bind you.

You Cannot Change What You Cannot See

A painter does not create blindly. A composer does not write music without first listening. A writer does not complete a novel without first reading what has been written. Likewise, your life cannot change until you first see it.

A basketball player reviews footage to refine his movement. A musician listens intently to each note to adjust his tone. The act of awareness—of paying attention—makes improvement possible. Without it, the same habits repeat. The same unconscious patterns continue. The same mistakes reappear, not because life is working against you, but because you are still reading the same page.

Bring awareness to your thoughts. Watch them as they arise. Do not resist them; do not push them away. Simply see them.

And in seeing, you begin to step beyond them.

Seeing the Patterns Beneath the Surface

Most people believe they are making choices, but in reality, they are reacting. They are operating on old programming, conditioned by their past, replaying the same struggles, thinking the same thoughts, and reinforcing the same limitations.

Do you notice certain themes in your life? Do you experience the same conflicts, fears, and resistance?

This is not life imposing itself upon you. This is the mind imposing itself upon life.

It is not the world that holds you captive—it is the lens through which you see it. The story repeats itself only because you have not yet seen it clearly.

When you do, something shifts. The space between thought and awareness grows. You begin to observe rather than react. And in this observation, you realize you are not bound by the past.

The story you have been living is just that—a story. And like all stories, it can be rewritten. But first, it must be seen.

Once you begin to see the patterns of the mind, something shifts. The illusion of permanence dissolves. And when the weight of past identity fades, freedom reveals itself—unnoticed, yet always present.

● ● ●

Self-awareness is not about fixing what is broken because nothing is broken—only unseen. The mind believes it must change, improve, and correct. However, true transformation does not happen through force or effort. It occurs through awareness.

When you bring presence to your life story, something shifts. You step outside of it. And when you step outside of it, you are no longer bound by it. The patterns, struggles, and limitations existed only because they went unnoticed.

So the question is not: *Can I change?*

The question is: *Am I willing to see?*

Real-World Examples of Awakening to One's Narrative

It is easy to believe that our past defines us and that the struggles we have endured are permanent rather than transient. But the past is only a thought—it does not exist in the present moment. What remains of it is only what the mind continues to carry.

Awakening is not an action—it is a realization. And in that realization, the self-imposed limits of the past dissolve. Some people awaken to this truth and, in doing so, step beyond the limitations of their conditioned self. The following are two examples of individuals who moved beyond their past and became conscious creators of their own narratives.

Case Study: Howard Schultz – From Struggle to Visionary

Howard Schultz did not inherit wealth, nor was he given a path that led naturally to success. He was born into poverty and raised in a Brooklyn public housing complex, watching his father struggle through unstable, low-wage jobs with no benefits. For many, such an experience becomes a fixed identity—a belief in limitation, scarcity, and hardship.

But identity is not reality. Identity is simply a story the mind tells itself.

Schultz did not accept the past as an unchangeable fact. Instead, he used it as fuel to consciously redefine his relationship with wealth, opportunity, and leadership.

» **Reframing Hardship** – Instead of viewing his childhood as an obstacle, he saw it as an initiation into resilience and empathy. He made it his mission to build a company that honored the dignity of its employees.

» **Redefining Identity** – He was not "born" a businessman. He became one by releasing the idea of who he was supposed to be and stepping into who he chose to become.

» **Owning the Narrative** – When investors doubted his vision, he remained steady. He understood that external resistance only reflects the internal doubts we have yet to transcend.

Key Points: Your past is only a memory. It is not who you are. The moment you see this, you step into a new reality.

Case Study: Bruce Lee – Beyond Limitation

Bruce Lee was not born into fame or success. When he arrived in the United States, he was met with skepticism, financial struggle, and resistance from a society that was not yet ready for him. Most people, when faced with such barriers, internalize them. They allow the limitations of the world to become the limitations of their mind.

But Bruce Lee did not accept limitation as truth. He did not see himself as a victim of circumstance. He saw himself as the creator of his own being.

» **Self-Definition** – He did not conform to the martial arts norms of the time. He transcended them, creating his philosophy: Jeet Kune Do.

» **Relentless Reinvention** – He did not resist obstacles. He flowed around them, adapting, refining, evolving. He understood that rigidity is limitation, while presence is infinite.

» **Breaking Barriers** – The world told him no, so he said yes. He was not reacting to life; he was moving through it consciously.

Reflection: What role are you playing in your own life? Are you accepting the script handed to you, or are you writing something new?

The Table of Contents Exercise: Seeing the Story of Your Life

A book is made of chapters, and so is your life. To become aware of your story, you must first see it clearly.

Not as something solid and unchanging but as something fluid that can be rewritten. When you see your life as a story, you begin to detach from it. You are no longer inside the book but looking at it. And from this place of awareness, you can create consciously rather than unconsciously.

Step 1: Name Your Chapters

Each phase of your life has a title.

Look back and observe:

» **Foundations** – The early years that shaped your beliefs.

» **Awakening** – A time when your perception began to shift.

» **Challenges** – The struggles that formed your identity.

» **Turning Point** – The moments that changed your trajectory.

» **Who I Am Now** – The story you are currently living.

Step 2: Recognize the Patterns

What themes have repeated? What beliefs have you carried with you?

Are they true or simply thoughts you have not yet questioned?

Step 3: Write the Next Chapter

Your past has already been written. But this moment is always new.

What comes next is yours to create.

...

A book does not define the reader.

Your life does not define you. The awareness that sees the story is beyond the story itself. The past has shaped you, but it is not who you are.

There is no past, no future—only now. And in the now, you are free.

Will you read unconsciously or awaken to the presence that sees?

Chapter Two

The Opening Lines – Early Life Influences

"We do not see things as they are; we see them as we are."

— Anaïs Nin

The First Pages: How Childhood Shapes Belief

Before you knew yourself as a name, before the mind created an identity, you were simply present. A child does not question existence—it simply is. There is no concept of the past, no worry about the future. Only now.

Yet, from the moment of birth, something begins to take shape: a story. Words are given to you; beliefs are handed down. You are told who you are, what the world is, and how things work. Like ink on a blank page, these early experiences form the first lines of your book.

At first, you do not question them. A child absorbs

everything, not as opinion but as reality. The voice of a parent, the structure of a home, and the emotions that fill the air are not seen as separate from the self. They are the self. A belief is not formed by choice but through unconscious repetition.

> **❮❮ You were given a story before you could choose one—but you are not bound to it. ❯❯**

You may have been told that the world is safe or that it is dangerous. That love is abundant or that it must be earned. That you are strong or that you are not enough. These messages, spoken or unspoken, become the framework through which you see yourself.

But here is the illusion: what you were given is not who you are. Unseen beliefs shape life. The past replays itself, unaware it is only words.

But when awareness arises, the first pages lose their power. You begin to see the story as just that—a story. The weight of old beliefs dissolves, and you recognize something deeper: you are not the past, nor the thoughts that came from it. You are the presence that sees.

And when you realize this, a space opens. A space where new words can be written. A space where you are no longer defined by the past but free in the eternal now.

Understanding the Stories You Inherited—From Parents, Culture, and Society

Before you had words of your own, there were words around you. Stories were spoken, repeated, reinforced—not as mere ideas, but as truth. These stories did not ask for your consent. They were absorbed, like air, shaping how you saw yourself and the world before you even knew you were looking.

Some of these stories came from your parents. Perhaps they told you that life is a struggle, that *love must be earned*, that success comes only through suffering. Or perhaps their stories were filled with warmth, encouragement, and abundance. But whether spoken directly or silently modeled through action, these early narratives became part of you—not because they were true, but because they were familiar.

Beyond your family, there was the culture you were born into. Every culture carries its own stories: who is valued, who is ignored, what is worthy, what is shameful. The mind absorbs these collective beliefs without questioning them, mistaking them for reality. What is considered normal, good, or possible is not universal—it is simply the conditioning of a particular place at a particular time. But unless you see this, the conditioning remains unseen.

Then, there is society itself. From childhood, you are taught how to fit into the structure that already exists. You are given roles, labels, and expectations. You are told what success looks like, what failure means, how you should think, and who you should become. These stories are so deeply embedded in human life that most people never realize they are living inside them. They believe they are free, but their thoughts, desires, and fears are shaped by a script they did not write.

But a story, no matter how convincing, is still only a story.

The moment awareness arises, the moment you see the inherited beliefs for what they are, they lose their grip. You realize that what you have been told is not the ultimate truth, only one version of it. The limitations you once accepted were not placed upon you by life itself but by unconscious conditioning.

And when you see this clearly, something shifts. A space opens between you and the inherited mind. In this space, you are no longer bound by the past. You are no longer acting out a role given to you by others.

You step beyond the story.

And in that stepping beyond, you return to something far deeper than belief: presence. Not a concept, not an identity—just being.

From this space, you are no longer shaped by the old narratives. You are free to choose, free to live, free to see the world—not as you were told it is, but as it is, in this moment.

Real-World Examples of Transmuting Pain into Purpose

Pain, when left unexamined, often becomes the foundation of identity. The experiences of hardship, trauma, and struggle can shape the way we see ourselves, making suffering feel like an inescapable reality rather than a passing chapter. But true empowerment does not come from denying the past—it comes from seeing it clearly and choosing not to be bound by it.

Some individuals take their pain and use it as a stepping stone, transforming it into a force for growth, connection, and purpose. The following is an example of someone who refused to let her past define her. Instead, she saw through the narrative of limitation and used her story to uplift not only herself but millions of others.

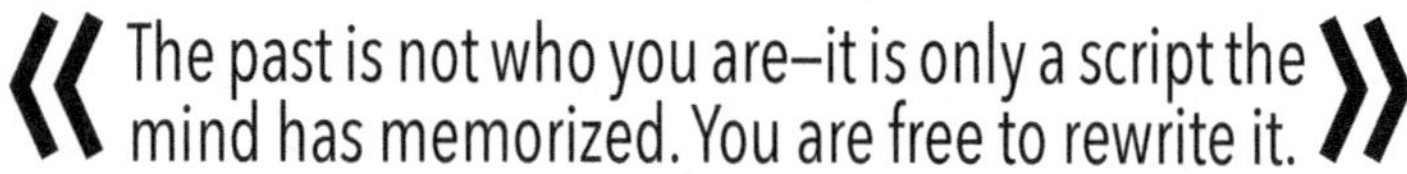

Case Study: Oprah Winfrey – Transforming an Abusive Childhood into a Platform for Empowerment

Pain is often mistaken for permanence. What happens to us in childhood seems to define us, shaping the mind's idea of who we are. But awareness reveals a deeper truth: pain is an experience, not an identity. The past is not who you are—it is only a story the mind repeats.

Oprah Winfrey's early life was filled with suffering. Born into poverty in rural Mississippi, she endured abuse, neglect, and profound hardship. In those years, she was given a story—a narrative of limitation, of struggle, of being unseen. Many would have remained within the walls of that identity, unconsciously reliving the past in new forms.

But something within her witnessed the story rather than becoming it.

From an early age, she discovered the power of voice. Speaking, reading, expressing—these were not just survival mechanisms but doorways into something greater. She saw that her past was not a life sentence but a lesson. The suffering she had endured did not define her—it awakened her to the suffering of others.

And in this awareness, transformation began.

» **Reframing Hardship** – Rather than internalizing the pain as her identity, she used it as a bridge to empathy. She recognized that her suffering allowed her to deeply understand the struggles of others.

» **Redefining Identity** – She was not trapped in the role the world had given her. She stepped beyond the conditioning of poverty, trauma, and societal limitation, creating herself anew.

» **Owning the Narrative** – The world told her who she

was supposed to be. Instead, she listened to something deeper. She became not only a storyteller but also a witness to the stories of others, providing a space for voices that were long silenced.

What could have remained a cycle of suffering became a platform for healing. Through television, writing, and philanthropy, she transformed personal pain into a collective awakening. She did not escape her past—she transmuted it, using it as a force for connection and empowerment.

Key Points: The past has no power unless you give it power. When you see your story from awareness rather than identification, suffering is no longer a weight—it is a doorway.

Oprah did not succeed in spite of her past. She succeeded because she saw beyond it.

The Preface Exercise: Writing a Summary of the Story You've Been Told About Yourself

A book begins with a preface—an introduction, a framing of what is to come. It tells the reader what to expect, shaping their perception before the story even begins.

Your life has a preface, too. But you did not write it.

Before you could form your own thoughts, before you could question, you were given a story. It came from your parents, your culture, your environment. You were told who you are, what is possible, and what is expected. Some of these messages were spoken aloud. Others were silent, embedded in actions, in the unspoken rules of your surroundings.

Without awareness, this preface becomes the lens through which you see yourself. It determines how you approach relationships, success, love, and failure. It creates an invisible boundary between what you believe you can do and what seems impossible.

But here is the truth: the preface is not the book. It is simply the introduction you were given.

You are free to rewrite it.

Step 1: Write Your Preface

Reflect on the messages you received about yourself growing up. What were you told—explicitly or implicitly—about:

> » **Who you are?** (Smart, not good enough, lovable, unworthy, strong, weak?)

> » **What you can or cannot do?** (You must follow the rules; you are meant for great things, you should not dream too big, life is hard, and success is for other people?)

> » **What love, success, and failure mean?** (Love must be earned, success requires struggle, failure defines you, and happiness is fleeting?)

Write a one-paragraph summary of the story you were given. Let it be honest, unfiltered.

Do not judge it—simply observe it.

Step 2: See It for What It Is

Now, step back and read what you wrote.

Ask yourself:

> » *Is this truly who I am, or is this what I was told to be?*

> » *Are these beliefs universal truths, or are they simply inherited thoughts?*

> » *If I were not holding onto this story, who would I be?*

In seeing the story, it loses its grip. It is no longer a reality—only words passing through awareness.

Step 3: Rewriting Your Preface

If you were to rewrite your introduction, what would it say?

What if, instead of limitation, it spoke of possibility? Instead of fear, it spoke of awareness. Instead of defining you by the past, it invited you into the present moment.

Take a moment. Write a new preface. One that aligns not with what you were told but with what you now see.

Exercise Reflection

A preface does not define a book—it is simply the first thing written. The story has not yet unfolded.

The next chapter is yours to write.

• • •

The first words of a book do not determine its ending. The past has shaped you, but it is not who you are. When awareness arises, the story loses its grip, and you step into something beyond it.

What would it feel like to no longer carry the weight of an inherited story?

Take a moment.

What beliefs from your early years can be released right now?

Chapter Three

Plot Points – Key Life Events

"Life is not what happens to you, but how you react to it."

— Epictetus

Recognizing the Turning Points That Have Shaped Your Character

Life does not move in a straight line. It unfolds, moment by moment, sometimes appearing to flow smoothly, other times shifting suddenly, altering the course of your path in ways you did not expect. These moments of change—some small, some profound—are what the mind calls turning points.

But what is a turning point, truly?

To the unconscious mind, it is something external—a major event, a loss, a success, a crisis. The mind labels it as good or bad, desirable or unfortunate. But this is only the surface.

The true turning point is not the event itself but the shift in awareness it brings.

When challenges arise, the mind resists—*"Why me?"* But what if they are not obstacles but invitations? It clings to what was, fearful of what is to come. But if awareness is present, something else emerges. You begin to see that the experience is not happening to you but for you—not as an external force shaping your life but as an invitation to awaken.

Think of a time in your life when everything changed. A loss, an achievement, an unexpected challenge. Was it the event that shaped you, or was it your response to it? Did it close you further into the conditioned mind, reinforcing fear and resistance? Or did it awaken something deeper, something that had always been there but had gone unnoticed?

This is the difference between being trapped in the story and seeing beyond it. The mind clings to the past, to what was, or it rushes ahead to what might be. But a true turning point happens only in the present moment. It is the moment when you stop resisting what is and instead bring awareness to it.

《 A turning point is not what happens to you— it is the moment you stop resisting what is. 》

There is no need to search for these moments or define them. They reveal themselves in stillness. Look back, not to analyze, but to see. Which experiences brought you deeper into unconsciousness, and which awakened you? And if awareness had been present in every moment—what would have changed?

When you recognize the turning points in your life not as

events but as awakenings, you realize that you were never shaped by them—you were only ever waking up.

How Major Life Events Influence Decision-Making and Personality

Life is not made of time; it is made of moments. Some pass unnoticed, like leaves carried by the wind. Others seem to hold weight, as if time itself had paused, demanding your attention. The mind calls these major life events—moments of change, challenge, or realization that appear to shape who you are.

But is it the event that shapes you, or is it the meaning you give to it?

To the unconscious mind, life happens to you. Events seem to impose themselves upon your path, forcing you to react, adapt, and become something different. A great loss, an unexpected success, a failure, a new beginning—each one leaves an imprint. The mind collects these experiences like chapters in a book, forming a narrative of identity: This is who I am. This is why I act this way. This is what life has taught me.

But the past is not shaping you—your attachment to it is.

A difficult experience does not make you fearful; the mind's resistance to that experience creates fear. A painful loss does not harden you; it is the ego's unwillingness to accept what is that builds walls around the heart. And success does not define you; it is only the mind clinging to a temporary outcome, mistaking achievement for identity.

Decision-making, too, is shaped in this way. Most choices are reactions to the past, not creations of the present. The mind recalls a painful experience and avoids risk. It remembers validation and seeks to repeat it. It projects old fears onto new situations, mistaking memory for wisdom.

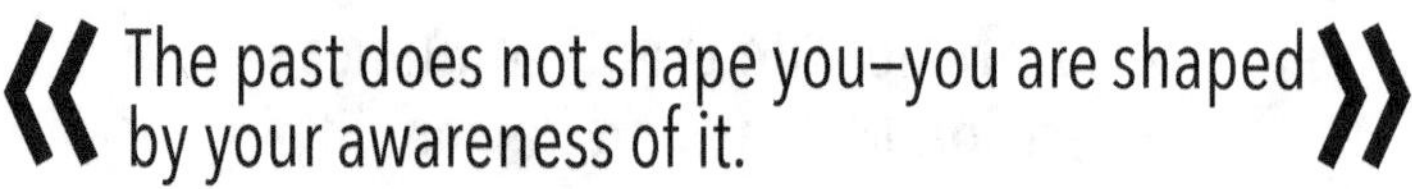

But awareness brings something new. When you become conscious, the past no longer dictates your choices. You begin to see that decisions do not need to come from fear or personality from old wounds. In presence, there is no past, no accumulation of experiences weighing you down—there is only this moment, fresh, unconditioned, free.

So ask yourself: Are you making decisions, or are your past experiences making them for you? Who would you be if you no longer carried the old story into every choice?

When you step into awareness, life no longer shapes you—you shape life.

Real-World Examples of Transforming Struggle into Strength

Hardship is often seen as a roadblock, something to overcome or escape. The mind resists struggle, believing that success and fulfillment come only when suffering ends. But what if struggle is not an obstacle, but an opening? What if it strips away illusions, forcing us to see what was always present beneath the surface?

True transformation does not come from avoiding pain, but from meeting it with awareness. The following is an example of someone who encountered adversity, not as a force working against her, but as an invitation to step into a greater version of herself. Through surrendering to the moment rather than resisting it, she was able to create something far greater than personal success—she created something that resonated with millions.

Case Study: J.K. Rowling – How Personal Struggles Became the Fuel for Her Success

The mind believes that suffering is an obstacle. It resists hardship, labels it as misfortune, and seeks to escape. But what if struggle is not a barrier but a doorway? What if the deepest challenges in life are not setbacks but invitations—to let go of resistance, to step beyond fear, to awaken to something greater?

The world often tells J.K. Rowling's story in terms of triumph: a struggling writer turned literary icon, a single mother who rose from poverty to unimaginable success. But to see only this external transformation is to miss the deeper truth: her journey was not just about perseverance—it was about presence.

At one point in her life, everything the mind clings to had fallen away. She was a single mother, unemployed, living in near poverty. To the world, it looked like failure. To the mind, it could have been a place of despair, fear, and self-doubt. But from within this space of nothingness, something emerged—a story, an idea, a world waiting to be written.

» **Reframing Hardship** – The suffering she experienced did not destroy her; it cleared away the distractions of the ego. Without the illusion of security, she was free to create—not for money or approval, but from a place of pure expression.

» **Redefining Identity** – She could have identified with struggle, reinforcing the belief that life was against her. Instead, she chose not to resist but to embrace the moment fully.

Writing became not an escape from pain but a movement through it.

» **Owning the Narrative** – Society might have told her that success was unlikely, that dreams were impractical. But she listened not to the world's doubts but the quiet knowing within. She followed the story as it unfolded without attachment to the outcome.

What could have remained a period of suffering became a turning point—not because she fought against hardship, but because she surrendered to the present. In embracing the now, creativity was allowed to flow freely.

Key Points: The mind sees struggle as an enemy. Awareness sees it as an opening. The greatest transformations do not come from escaping pain but from allowing it to dissolve in presence.

J.K. Rowling did not rise above her past—she stepped beyond it. And in doing so, she created something that existed beyond her: a story that awakened something in millions of others.

Case Study: Malala Yousafzai - Overcoming Adversity and Rewriting Her Life's Purpose After Trauma

The mind believes that trauma defines us. It clings to pain, forms an identity around suffering, and mistakes the past for the present. But awareness reveals something deeper: what happens to you does not make you who you are—your response to it does.

Malala Yousafzai's story is often told as one of defiance and bravery, a young girl who stood up for education and survived an attack meant to silence her. But the deeper truth is not about resistance—it is about presence. She did not let adversity harden her. She did not let trauma consume her. She did not allow fear to shape her destiny. Instead, she stepped beyond the story of what happened to her and into something far greater: purpose.

When Malala was shot for speaking out, the world might have expected her to retreat into fear. To shrink back, to remain silent. The mind, conditioned by survival, often reacts in this way—pulling away from risk, avoiding pain, seeking safety in invisibility.

But awareness does not shrink; it expands.

» **Reframing Hardship** – She could have seen her experience as confirmation that the world is cruel, that fear must dictate her actions. Instead, she saw it as proof of something else: that her voice mattered. That truth is stronger than fear.

» **Redefining Identity** – She could have become a victim, allowing trauma to define her. But she did not hold onto what happened—she stepped beyond it. She did not see herself as broken but as a force for change.

» **Owning the Narrative** – The world told her to be silent. Instead, she spoke louder. Not from anger, not from revenge, but from clarity. She did not fight against what happened—she transformed it into a movement that reached beyond herself.

She did not return to the life she had before—because the past was gone. Instead, she moved fully into the present, where she was no longer just Malala, the girl who had been attacked, but Malala, the voice of millions.

Key Points: Trauma does not define you; your awareness of it does. You are not what happens to you—you are what remains when the past dissolves.

Malala did not let her suffering become her identity. She let it become her awakening. And in doing so, she not only changed her own life—she changed the world.

The Timeline Exercise: Mapping Out Key Events That Have Defined Your Journey

Life is not a straight path; it is a series of moments—some barely noticed, others so powerful they seem to divide time into before and after. The mind remembers these moments as key events, believing they shaped who you are. But it is not the events themselves that define you—it is the awareness you bring to them.

The purpose of this exercise is not to relive the past nor to judge it but to see it clearly. When you bring awareness to the turning points in your life, you step outside of the story and begin to recognize something deeper: you were never shaped by these events—you were only ever waking up.

Step 1: Identifying the Key Events in Your Life

Reflect on the defining moments that have shaped your journey. These may be events that brought great change, joy, loss, or realization.

Some examples:

» A childhood experience that shaped your sense of self.

» A moment of deep loss or struggle.

» A success or breakthrough that shifted your perspective.

» A time when you made a life-altering decision.

» A moment when your perception of the world changed.

Write down at least five key moments in your life. Do not analyze them—simply record them.

Step 2: Observing the Patterns

Now, look at your timeline. Ask yourself:

» Do you see recurring themes in these events?

» Are there patterns in how you responded to challenges or success?

» Were these moments shaping you, or were they simply revealing something that was already there?

Awareness arises not when we resist the past but when we see it without judgment.

Step 3: Reframing Your Story

For each event, write one sentence describing how your mind has interpreted it. Then, write a second sentence from awareness—how would you see this moment if you were no longer attached to the story?

Example:

» **Mind's Story:** *"That failure proved I wasn't good enough."*

» **Awareness:** *"That experience showed me that failure is not who I am, only something that happened."*

Do this for each event. As you do, notice: Is there space between you and the story now?

Step 4: Seeing the Timeline for What It Is

Your past may seem like a series of cause-and-effect moments leading you to where you are. But the past is only memory, and memory exists only in thought. The only thing that has ever been real is this moment.

If the past does not define you, then who are you now—without the weight of what has been?

Take a breath. Look at your timeline again. What if, instead of shaping you, these events had only been pointing you back to presence?

Exercise Reflection

A timeline is not a destiny. It is not a fixed path that led you here.

It is just a story.

And like all stories, it can be seen for what it is—words on a page. You are not the words. You are the awareness that sees them.

· · ·

Your life's turning points are not just events; they are opportunities for transformation. How you interpret them will determine whether they hold you back or propel you forward. What would it feel like to no longer carry the weight of an inherited story?

Take a moment. What beliefs from your early years can be released right now?

Chapter Four

Character Development – Who You Are and Who You've Become

"Who looks outside, dreams; who looks inside, awakes."

— Carl Jung

Analyzing Your Character Arc–The Strengths, Weaknesses, and Personality Traits You've Developed

Who you believe yourself to be is a story—a collection of memories, experiences, and interpretations the mind has gathered over time. It weaves a narrative: *This is who I am. These are my strengths. These are my weaknesses.* But is this true, or is it simply a pattern of thought?

The mind identifies with its story. It clings to past successes and failures, shaping an image of self. You may see yourself as strong, independent, intelligent, or resilient. Or perhaps you identify with limitations: *I am anxious. I am not good enough. I always struggle with change.* These identities feel real because they have been repeated, reinforced, and left unquestioned. But if you were to pause for a moment and ask: *Who am I without these thoughts?*—*what remains?*

The story of your life may have highs and lows, victories and setbacks, but none of these define you. The traits you believe you have developed—whether you call them strengths or weaknesses—are not who you are; they are only roles the mind has played.

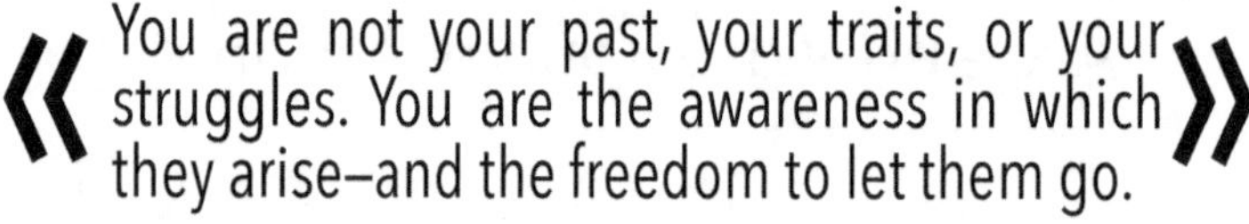

Look at your so-called strengths. Do they arise from presence, or are they a defense mechanism built to protect an identity? Is confidence a natural expression or a reaction to past insecurity? Is resilience the ability to stay present, or is it an attachment to struggle?

Now, look at what you perceive as weaknesses. Are they real limitations, or are they simply thoughts that have been believed? What happens when you stop labeling yourself as impatient, fearful, or unworthy? Do these qualities dissolve when no longer reinforced by identity?

Your transformation is not about change but release. The true transformation is not in becoming someone different but in realizing you were never the story to begin with.

Who are you without the labels?

In the stillness of this moment, beyond thought, beyond identity—you are.

Understanding the Protagonist's Journey–Where You've Been and Where You're Headed

The mind sees life as a journey—a path unfolding through time, moving from past to future, from where you were to where you are going. It tells a story of progress, of struggle, of becoming. But is this journey real, or is it simply a narrative created by thought?

To the unconscious mind, you are the protagonist of this story. You have a past that defines you and a future that awaits you. You have goals to achieve, obstacles to overcome, and a path that seems to stretch ahead. The mind is always looking forward or looking back, believing that life is something happening to you, something you must navigate, control, or improve.

But what if there is no journey—only this moment?

Where have you been? The past is nothing more than memory, a collection of thoughts arising now. The experiences you believe shaped you are only stories the mind retells. They feel real because you have given them meaning, but they are no longer here.

Where are you going? The future is an imagined destination, a projection of thought. The mind creates an identity around who you will become—wiser, stronger, more fulfilled. It believes happiness, success, or peace will come later. But later is just another thought, and the self you are striving to become is only an illusion of time.

In reality, there is no past defining you, no future waiting for you—there is only now.

The true journey is not about moving forward but about

awakening to what has always been present. It is not about becoming but about being.

> **The greatest transformations do not come from changing who you are, but from realizing you were never the story to begin with.**

The more you release the idea of a self traveling through time, the more you recognize that you are not the protagonist—you are the awareness in which all stories arise and dissolve.

So instead of asking, *Where am I headed?*

Ask: *Am I fully here?*

Real-World Example of Finding Freedom in Confinement

The mind equates suffering with limitation. It believes that adversity diminishes power, that true freedom exists only when external conditions change. But history has shown that real freedom is not found in circumstances—it is found in presence. Some individuals experience hardship not as a prison, but as a crucible, burning away ego, resentment, and attachment until only clarity remains.

The following is an example of a leader who faced decades of confinement yet emerged not hardened by suffering, but transformed by it. His journey reveals that true strength is not about resistance, but about surrender—not to oppression, but to the realization that no external force can define who you are.

Case Study: Nelson Mandela – How Years of Imprisonment Shaped Him into a Transformational Leader

The mind resists suffering. It sees hardship as something to escape, as an injustice to fight against. It believes that freedom exists somewhere beyond the present moment, somewhere outside of pain.

But true freedom is not found in changing external circumstances—it is found in surrendering to what is.

Nelson Mandela's life could have been a story of bitterness, of anger, of a man hardened by injustice. Sentenced to life in prison for his resistance against apartheid, he was placed behind bars for 27 years. The mind would say this was a loss—a stripping away of power, movement, control. But something else happened. Instead of becoming consumed by resentment, he awakened to a deeper truth: his captors could imprison his body, but not his presence.

» **Reframing Hardship** – Prison did not break him; it dissolved the illusion that his power depended on external freedom. In the stillness of confinement, he discovered a deeper strength—not through resistance, but through acceptance.

» **Redefining Identity** – He entered prison as a revolutionary; he emerged as a statesman. His time in solitude stripped away the ego's need for vengeance and revealed a leader not ruled by the past but by clarity.

» **Owning the Narrative** – The world expected him to seek retaliation. Instead, he forgave. His suffering became the foundation for his wisdom, and his greatest act of defiance was not revenge but peace.

Many would have remained trapped—if not by the prison walls, then by their own mind. But Mandela saw beyond the story of injustice, beyond the need to prove, beyond the illusion of separation. He stepped out of prison not just as a free man but as a man who had always been free.

Key Points: The greatest transformations do not happen through struggle but through surrender. True power is not found in control but in presence.

Nelson Mandela did not become great because of his suffering. He became great because he no longer identified with it. And in doing so, he did not just free himself—he freed a nation.

Self-Assessment Exercises – Personality Tests, Journaling Prompts, and Reflection Questions

The mind loves to define itself. It seeks to categorize, measure, and place itself within a framework of strengths and weaknesses. It asks, *Who am I?* and searches for answers in personality tests, labels, and identities. But is this true self-knowledge, or just another layer of thought?

The purpose of self-assessment is not to confirm who you think you are but to observe the mind without identifying with it. The moment you define yourself, you create a boundary, a limitation. True self-awareness is not about finding answers—it is about seeing beyond the questions.

• • •

The following exercises designed not to reinforce identity but to bring awareness to the self you have constructed—and the presence that exists beyond it.

Self-Observation: Witnessing the Conditioned Self

For one day, observe your reactions to people, situations, and challenges.

Do not judge them—simply notice:

» When do you feel the need to defend yourself?

» When do you seek approval?

» When do you become impatient, anxious, or frustrated?

» Who are you when no one is watching?

Each of these reactions is part of a conditioned self—a personality built on past experiences and beliefs. Are these reactions truly who you are, or are they patterns the mind has created?

Journaling Prompts: Observing the Story of "Me"

Write freely, without filtering or overthinking. Allow whatever arises to appear on the page.

» *What stories do I tell myself about who I am? (Am I strong? Am I not enough? Am I always struggling?)*

» *Who would I be without these stories?*

» *What fears keep me attached to my current identity?*

» *When in my life have I felt completely present, without needing to define myself?*

Do not look for the "right" answers. Just notice what the mind clings to and what happens when you step beyond it.

Reflection Questions: Seeing Through the Illusion of Personality

Do not answer these questions. Sit with them. Let them dissolve.

» *If I could no longer use words to describe myself, who would I be?*

» *If I let go of every role—friend, parent, leader, student— what remains?*

> » *What part of my identity am I most afraid to lose? Why?*
>
> » *What happens when I stop trying to improve myself and simply allow myself to be?*

The mind may resist these questions, searching for definitions for something solid to hold onto. But who you are is not found in words nor in thought. It is found in the space between them.

When the need to define yourself fades, what is left is presence.

• • •

Characters evolve based on the choices they make. The person you are today is the sum of your experiences, but the person you become is up to you.

What strengths have emerged from your challenges? How will you use them moving forward? If character is only a story, then who are you without it? In this moment, what remains?

Chapter Five

The Story You Tell Yourself & the Roles You Play

"The world isn't just the way it is. It is how we understand it."

— Paulo Coelho

Your Life's Genre – Drama, Comedy, Adventure, or Something Else?

The mind is a storyteller. It creates meaning out of events, assigns roles to people, and constructs a narrative about who you are. It tells you that your life has a genre—perhaps a tragedy, a comedy, an adventure. It convinces you that you are the protagonist, that the plot is unfolding in a certain way, and that your past and future are chapters leading somewhere.

But is this true, or is it simply another illusion?

Look at the story you tell yourself. Do you see your life as a struggle, a series of challenges that must be overcome? The mind may call this a drama, full of conflict, obstacles, and suffering, or perhaps you see life as an adventure, where new experiences unfold, and each moment is an opportunity for discovery. Maybe you view it as a comedy, a collection of absurdities and unexpected turns that remind you not to take anything too seriously.

But what if life has no genre at all?

The idea that your life fits into a category is simply another mental construct. It is an attempt to give structure to something that is ultimately formless.

A genre is only a lens, a way of interpreting events through conditioned thought. If you believe your life is a tragedy, you will find evidence to support this belief. If you believe it is an adventure, the same applies. But the truth is, life itself is beyond definition—it is simply unfolding, moment by moment.

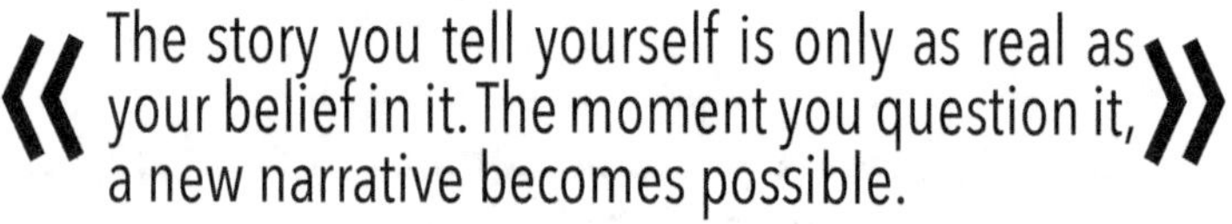

Without the story, who remains?

When you stop labeling your life, you step into something deeper—presence. In presence, there is no drama, no comedy, no adventure—only the now. The moment you stop seeing yourself as a character, you realize you are something much greater: the awareness in which all stories arise and fade away.

So instead of asking, *What kind of story am I living?*, ask:

Am I fully here, beyond the story?

The Supporting Cast – How Relationships Shape Your Self-Identity

The mind creates identity not in isolation but through relationships. It defines itself in contrast to others—friend, partner, parent, teacher, student. Each role reinforces a sense of self, a character in the unfolding story of me. The people around you become the supporting cast, reflecting back an image of who you believe yourself to be.

But is this image real, or is it simply a role you have learned to play?

The unconscious mind seeks validation through relationships. It looks to others to confirm its identity: *Am I lovable? Am I important? Am I seen?* When people respond in ways that reinforce these beliefs, the mind feels secure. When they challenge or reject them, the mind reacts—defending, blaming, withdrawing.

This is the trap of identification: seeing yourself only through the eyes of others.

Yet, no relationship can truly define you because who you are is not a role—it is the awareness behind all roles. The way others perceive you is filtered through their own conditioning, their own narratives.

Their approval or disapproval, their praise or criticism— none of it is about you. It is only a reflection of their own mind.

So, how do relationships shape identity? They do not shape who you are, but they do reveal where you are still attached. If someone's words can make you feel unworthy, it is because there is still a part of you that believes in that unworthiness. If someone's rejection causes suffering, it is because the mind has placed identity in being accepted. Relationships, then, become an opportunity—not to reinforce who you think you are, but to see through the illusion of self entirely.

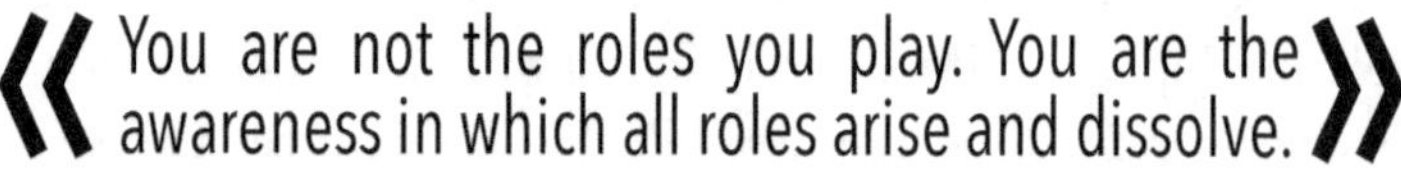

When you stop looking to others to confirm your identity, relationships shift. They are no longer a means of validation but an experience of presence. You no longer need to play a role—you simply are. And in that stillness, true connection arises—not between two separate selves, but in the shared awareness beyond identity.

So instead of asking, *Who am I in this relationship?*, ask:

What remains when all roles are dropped?

Real-World Examples of Identity and Reinvention

It is easy to believe that who we are is fixed, shaped by our past experiences, societal roles, and external perceptions. But identity is not a rigid construct—it is a fluid narrative, constantly evolving as we awaken to deeper self-awareness. The stories we tell ourselves can confine us or set us free. True transformation does not come from forcing change but from recognizing that identity itself is a construct, one that can be rewritten or even transcended.

The following are two examples of individuals who faced defining moments in their lives—moments that challenged their sense of self and forced them to either cling to an old identity or step into something greater. Their journeys reveal the power of reinvention, not as a form of escape, but as an awakening to what has always been true beyond the roles they once played.

The mind clings to identity. It builds an image of self, crafted through past experiences, achievements, and how others perceive us. It says *This is who I am*. But what happens when that image begins to dissolve? When the role you have played no longer fits, and the world no longer sees you the way you once saw yourself?

Case Study: Will Smith – His Journey of Rewriting His Public and Personal Identity

Will Smith's life has been a continuous process of self-reinvention. From rapper to sitcom star, from action hero to Oscar-winning actor, his public identity has evolved many times. But beneath these transformations, something deeper was unfolding—not just a career shift, but a confrontation with the illusion of self.

For much of his life, success was his foundation. Like many, he built an identity around achievement, external validation, and public approval. His charisma, humor, and larger-than-life presence were not just natural expressions but carefully maintained aspects of the persona he had created. The world saw him as confident, unstoppable—a man who could turn anything into gold. And yet, beneath the surface, there was something else: a quiet but growing awareness that no amount of success could bring true fulfillment.

Then came a moment of reckoning. A single action, played out on the world stage, shattered the image. The carefully constructed persona—so controlled, so likable—was suddenly in question. The mind resists such moments, grasping for explanations and justifications, a way to preserve the old identity.

But if presence arises, something else happens: surrender. The realization that the image was never real to begin with.

» **Reframing Identity** – Will Smith had spent decades crafting who he thought he was. But identity is not built—it is seen through. His personal crisis became an opportunity not to repair his image but to recognize its impermanence.

» **Letting Go of External Validation** – For years, his sense of self was shaped by applause, by public perception. However, no identity that depends on others can be real. The fall from admiration to scrutiny was not a punishment—it was an awakening.

» **Moving Beyond the Role** – The world will always try to define you. But when you no longer need to be seen a certain way, you become free. True transformation does not happen when you rebuild the mask but when you no longer need to wear one.

In every life, there comes a moment when the story you have told yourself begins to unravel. The mind will want to grasp at it, to rewrite it in a way that feels comfortable and controlled.

But real freedom is not in rewriting—it is in stepping beyond the story entirely.

Key Points: Who you are is not your reputation. Not your achievements. Not how the world sees you. The true self is not something that needs to be protected or restored—it is what remains when the illusion of self is no longer needed.

Will Smith did not just face a crisis of public identity—he faced an invitation to let go. And in that letting go, something deeper emerges: not a new version of self, but the awareness that has always been there.

The mind creates roles, assigning them based on culture, upbringing, and the expectations of others. It tells you who you are, where you belong, and how you must act to be accepted.

But what happens when you do not fit into a role? When your very existence challenges the structures society has built?

Case Study: Trevor Noah – Navigating Social Roles and Expectations in Extreme Circumstances

Trevor Noah was born into a world where identity was dictated by law. Under apartheid South Africa, race was not just a social construct—it was a system of control. Being mixed-race in a country where racial categories were rigid meant that he did not belong anywhere. Too light-skinned to be Black, too dark-skinned to be White, his very presence was an anomaly, an offense to a system that sought to define people by labels.

The mind resists uncertainty. It seeks to belong, a place to fit in, and a role to play. However, for Trevor Noah, there was no obvious role. In childhood, this could have been a source of suffering—an internal battle to belong, to be accepted by a society that saw him as "wrong." But something else happened. Rather than becoming trapped in the struggle to fit in, he learned to move between roles, to see identity not as something fixed but as something fluid.

» **Shifting Between Worlds** – In a country where race dictated one's place, Trevor Noah became adaptable. He learned languages, accents, and cultural nuances, moving between different groups, never fully belonging but always observing.

» **Seeing Through the Illusion of Identity** – He recognized that race, class, and social expectations were not absolute truths but constructs—systems created by human thought. And if they were constructs, they could not define him.

» **Humor as Presence** – Rather than resisting his circumstances, he embraced them. Comedy became a way to expose the absurdity of identity labels, to bring lightness to the weight of history, and to dissolve the divisions that the mind clings to.

Most people seek to define themselves within rigid roles, believing that security comes from certainty. But Trevor Noah's life revealed a deeper truth—identity itself is fluid, and freedom arises when labels dissolve.

He was neither fully one thing nor another—and in that, he became free.

Key Points: The roles society gives you are not who you are. The mind will try to fit you into a category, to define you in a way that feels safe, predictable. But when you stop seeking validation through labels, something else arises: freedom.

Trevor Noah's journey was not about finding where he belonged—it was about realizing that belonging itself is an illusion. When you no longer seek an identity, you discover what has always been there: the awareness beyond all roles.

The Narrative Shift Exercise – Changing Limiting Personal Stories into Empowering Ones

The mind tells stories. It weaves together memories, emotions, and past experiences, shaping a narrative of who you are and what is possible for you. These stories become the foundation of your identity: *I am this kind of person. Life has always been this way for me. This is what I can or cannot do.*

But what if these stories are not reality—only thoughts

that have been repeated and believed? What if the limits they impose are only as real as your attachment to them?

The Narrative Shift Exercise is not about replacing one story with another. It is about seeing through the illusion of the story itself—recognizing that who you are is not the story but the awareness in which all stories arise and dissolve.

Step 1: Identify the Story You've Been Telling Yourself

Take a moment to reflect on a belief that has shaped your life. Write it down as a single statement.

Some examples:

- » I always struggle with relationships.
- » I am not good enough.
- » I never finish what I start.
- » Success is for other people, not me.
- » I am always anxious in new situations.

This is the narrative the mind has constructed. It may feel true because it has been repeated, reinforced, and accepted without question. But truth is not in repetition—truth is in direct experience, in what is present right now.

Step 2: Observe the Story Without Identifying With It

Now, step back and look at what you wrote.

Ask yourself:

- » *Is this story happening right now, in this moment?*
- » *Who would I be if I no longer believed this thought?*
- » *Is this a fact, or just a conditioned belief shaped by the past?*

Notice how the mind wants to defend the story. It may

look for evidence to prove it right. But awareness does not need proof—it simply sees.

Can you observe the thought without attaching to it? Can you feel the space between you and the belief?

Step 3: Shift from Story to Presence

Let the story dissolve. Sit in the stillness beyond it, where the old narrative does not exist. Breathe. Notice the stillness. From this place of awareness, write a new statement—not a forced affirmation, but a reflection of what is true beyond the story.

Examples:

> » Relationships are experienced in the present, not shaped by the past.

> » I am here, complete as I am.

> » The moment I bring awareness to what I start, I move forward naturally.

> » Success is not an identity—it is a moment-by-moment unfolding.

> » Anxiety is only a thought, and in presence, it has no power.

Do not try to convince yourself—just allow these words to emerge from a place of stillness.

Step 4: Live Without the Story

For one day, practice being without the old narrative. The mind may try to bring it back—notice this without judgment. Each time the thought arises, simply ask:

> » *Is this happening right now, or is it just a thought?*

> » *Who am I without this belief?*

You do not need to force change. The story loses power not when you replace it but when you stop identifying with it.

Exercise Reflection

The mind will always tell stories. It will try to define you, limit you, shape you into something it can understand. But the truth of who you are is not in a story—it is in the space beyond thought.

So, instead of asking, *How can I change my story?* Ask:

Who am I when the story fades?

• • •

The roles you play in life are not your identity. You are the storyteller, not the story. If the mind no longer clings to a role, what remains?

Without definition, is anything lost?

Chapter Six

Your Story's Setting – How Environment Shapes Your Narrative

"You are the average of the five people you spend the most time with."

—Jim Rohn

Your Story's Setting – How Your Environment Influences Your Thoughts, Emotions, and Choices

The mind believes that who you are is shaped by where you are. It looks at your surroundings—your home, your culture, the people around you—and says, This is my story. This is what I have become because of my circumstances. It creates an identity out of environment, believing that external conditions determine inner experience.

But does your setting truly define you, or is it simply the backdrop against which the mind projects its narrative?

❰❰ You are not where you are. You are who you choose to be, wherever you stand. ❱❱

Surroundings may trigger thought, but they do not create it. A busy city may invite restlessness, just as a quiet landscape may encourage stillness. But these experiences are not caused by the place itself—they are interpretations made by the mind. One person may find peace in solitude; another may find discomfort. One may feel inspired by a bustling city; another may feel overwhelmed.

The setting is the same; only perception changes.

The mind is conditioned to seek meaning in environment, attaching identity to where you were born, the people you were raised around, or the culture that surrounds you. *It says I am this way because of where I come from.* But the truth is, who you are is not shaped by your environment—only the thoughts you believe about it.

Look at your surroundings. Do you see them as limitations? Do you believe they are responsible for your happiness or suffering? Or can you recognize that no external setting holds power over you—only your identification with it does?

When awareness arises, the setting no longer dictates the story. The environment remains, but it is seen for what it is— neutral, impermanent, part of the ever-changing flow of life. No place, no situation, no condition can define you. You are not where you are. You are here.

So instead of asking, *How has my environment shaped me?*

Ask: *Who am I, wherever I am?*

The Impact of Culture, Relationships, and Societal Expectations on Self-Perception

From the moment you are born, the world begins to tell you who you are. Before you can question, before you can choose, you inherit identities—through culture, through family, through the silent rules of society. The mind absorbs these as unquestioned truths: *This is how I should be. This is what is expected of me. This is who I am.*

But are these identities real, or are they just roles the mind has accepted?

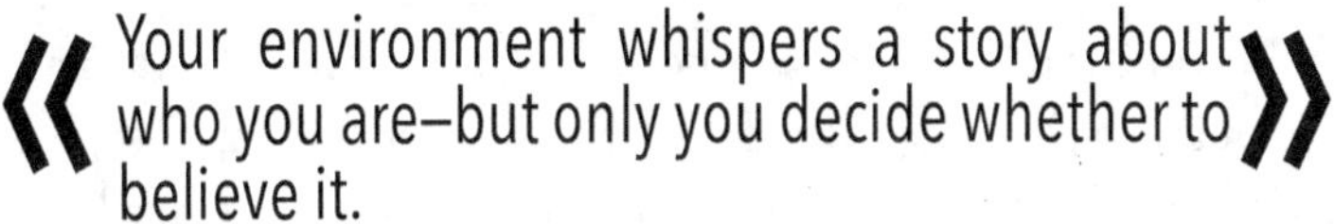

Culture defines what is considered normal, valuable, or worthy. It tells you how to behave, what to believe, and what success looks like. Society reinforces this with approval or rejection, rewarding conformity, and discouraging deviation. Relationships reflect these expectations back to you—who you are as a friend, a partner, a parent, a student. The self you believe yourself to be is shaped by these external forces, conditioned by the expectations of others.

But who are you without them?

If you were born in another place, raised by different people, and immersed in another culture, would you be the same person? Or would the story change, molded by different rules and different beliefs? If identity shifts based on external factors, can it ever be who you truly are?

Self-perception is not reality—it is a reflection of

conditioning. The moment you begin to see this, something shifts. You realize that no label, no expectation, no cultural framework can define you. You are not what society has told you to be. You are not even who you think you are.

You are the awareness that sees beyond all of it.

So instead of asking, *How do others see me?*

Ask: *Who am I beyond what I have been told?*

Real-World Examples of Vision Beyond Circumstance

Many believe that success is a product of environment—that the right conditions, the right mentors, or the right opportunities create extraordinary individuals. But true visionaries are not shaped by their surroundings; they are revealed through them. They do not simply react to setbacks or external influences; they transcend them, using both success and failure as stepping stones toward something greater.

The following is an example of someone who did not allow circumstances—neither privilege nor adversity—to define him. Instead, he used every experience, every challenge, and every loss as an opportunity to strip away illusion and step into deeper clarity. His story is not just one of innovation but of surrender—the ability to let go of identity, embrace the unknown, and see what others could not.

The mind believes that external conditions shape identity, that a person becomes who they are because of where they are and what happens to them. It looks at the setting of a life— circumstances, culture, setbacks—and says, This is why they succeeded. This is why they failed. But what if challenges and environments do not create vision but only reveal it?

Case Study: Steve Jobs – How Environment and Personal Setbacks Shaped His Visionary Thinking

Steve Jobs was born into a world of innovation. Raised in Silicon Valley, he was surrounded by technological breakthroughs and by people who questioned the limits of what was possible. The mind might say this environment shaped his destiny and that he became a visionary because he was immersed in a world of visionaries. But many people grew up in the same place, under the same conditions. Not all of them saw the world as he did.

So, was it the setting that shaped him, or was it his ability to see beyond it?

For Jobs, setbacks were not roadblocks—they were moments of awakening. Being fired from Apple, the very company he had built, could have been a failure. But instead of resisting it, he surrendered to what was. He later described it as "one of the best things that ever happened" to him. Why? Because it forced him to let go of identity and detach from the role the mind had created. He was no longer the young genius leading a revolution. He was simply a man, standing at the edge of the unknown.

And in that space, vision was allowed to unfold.

» **The Influence of Silicon Valley** – His environment exposed him to innovation, but he was not shaped by it. Instead, he used it as a canvas, seeing possibilities that others overlooked.

» **Setbacks as Awakening** – Instead of resisting failure, he allowed it to strip away the ego, making space for a deeper clarity to emerge.

» **Seeing Beyond the Known** – He understood that the greatest ideas are not created—they are uncovered. Presence, not effort, allows true vision to arise.

Many would have remained trapped in the story—either by success or by failure. But Jobs moved beyond both. His thinking was not shaped by environment or setbacks but by his ability to detach from them. He did not allow his surroundings to define him. Instead, he used them as a mirror, a way to see beyond what was and into what could be.

Key Points: Your setting does not define you. Setbacks only reveal where you are still holding on. When you stop resisting what is, the mind's limitations fall away. What remains is vision—not of the future, but of what is already here, waiting to be seen.

Steve Jobs did not create his success. He surrendered to it. And in that surrender, the future unfolded.

The Scene Change Exercise – Identifying and Adjusting Environmental Factors That Hold You Back

The mind believes that change must come from within. It tells you that no matter where you are, no matter what surrounds you, you should simply adapt. But what if your environment is not just a backdrop but an active part of the story your mind is creating?

The places you spend your time, the people you surround yourself with, the noise that fills your day—these are not just details. They shape your thoughts, your emotions, your sense of self. A chaotic environment breeds a disorganized mind. A stagnant setting reinforces a stagnant narrative.

The question is not just *What do I believe about myself?* But also, *Where am I, and how does this place reinforce that belief?*

This exercise is not about escaping your environment. It is

about seeing it clearly, recognizing where it influences you unconsciously, and making changes—not to control life, but to remove the barriers that keep you from presence.

Step 1: Observe Your Environment Without Judgment

For one day, notice. Do not try to change anything—observe.

> » How does the space around you feel? Does it create stillness or restlessness?

> » What sounds fill your world? Are they supportive of presence or distractions?

> » Who do you interact with most? Do these interactions pull you into unconscious patterns or bring clarity?

Your surroundings are more than physical—they are an extension of thought, shaping perception moment by moment. Can you see where they influence you without defining you?

Step 2: Identify What No Longer Serves You

Once you have observed, begin to question.

> » Are there places you go that drain you rather than energize you?

> » Are there habits in your space that reinforce old, limiting narratives?

> » Are there relationships that keep you bound to a role you no longer wish to play?

The mind resists change. It says *This is just the way things are.*

But is that true? Or is it simply conditioning?

Step 3: Adjust with Awareness, Not Force

Instead of changing the environment, shift your awareness first. See how space opens when presence arises.

> » If your space is cluttered, remove one thing that no longer aligns with you.

> » If noise fills your day, create one moment of silence.

> » If certain interactions leave you feeling disconnected, spend less time in them.

It is not about controlling your environment—it is about stepping out of unconscious patterns and seeing what happens when space is created.

Step 4: Experience the Shift

For one week, make one environmental adjustment and notice what changes—not just in your surroundings, but in your state of being.

> » Do you feel lighter? More present? Less reactive?

> » Are thoughts arising with more clarity?

> » Does removing external noise make the inner stillness more noticeable?

The shift does not come from forcing new habits or moving to a new place. It comes from seeing clearly what has been shaping you and making room for something different.

Exercise Reflection

Your environment does not define you, but it does influence the mind. The question is not whether you should change where you are but whether you can be fully here, wherever you are—and whether minor adjustments can create the space for presence to emerge.

Instead of asking, *What do I need to fix?* Ask:

What can I release?

· · ·

Your environment is like the backdrop of a novel, but you are not the story—you are the awareness in which it unfolds.

Does your current setting support the narrative you want to create? If not, what small change can you make today to align your surroundings with your highest potential?

We'd Love to Hear From You!

Thank you so much for reading this book-it means the world to me. If you found it helpful, inspiring, or just enjoyable, would you take a moment to leave a review? Your feedback not only helps others but also keeps me motivated to create more valuable content for you.

Here's how you can leave a review:

1. Scan the QR code on this page to go directly to the author's page.

2. Or, visit your Amazon Orders page, find this book, and click "Write a Product Review."

Your kind words make a big difference.
Thank you for your support!

PART TWO

Reading Between the Lines

"Until you make the unconscious conscious, it will direct your life and you will call it fate."

—C.G. Jung

Not everything in a book is written in bold letters. Some of the most important messages are hidden between the lines. The same is true for your life. The way you think, feel, and act is influenced by unconscious beliefs, patterns, and recurring themes you may not even realize are shaping your choices.

This section will help you become a better reader of your own life, uncovering the invisible scripts that direct your decisions so that you can take control of your narrative.

Chapter Seven

Reading Between the Lines - Understanding Your Unconscious Mind

"Your thoughts become your reality."

— Buddha

The Illusion of the Hidden Subtext

A silent force moves beneath your daily life, shaping your thoughts and emotions. Unnoticed, it influences your choices, reactions, and perception of reality.

This is the hidden subtext of the mind.

Like the roots of a tree hidden beneath the soil, unseen forces shape the way you grow and the way you move through life. It is made of old conditioning, absorbed beliefs, and unconscious fears. It is the voice that whispers, *"This is who I am. This is how life works. This is what I must do."* But these are not your original thoughts. They echo the past—things learned, repeated, and believed without question.

Perhaps you were told, *"Life is a struggle."* And so, struggle becomes the lens through which you see everything. Perhaps you absorbed the idea that *"I must prove my worth."* And so, you move through life in a state of tension, always chasing something just out of reach. The subtext is invisible, but its influence is everywhere.

> « You are not your thoughts. You are the awareness that sees them arise and dissolve, like waves upon the shore. »

When you are unaware of this hidden layer, you mistake it for reality. You believe you are simply responding to life, unaware that you are responding to a story written long ago. But here is the truth: the subtext is not life itself—it is only a mental interpretation of life.

The moment you see this clearly, something shifts. A space opens. You begin to notice the thoughts before they turn into emotions, and the assumptions before they become reactions. You recognize that you are not bound by them.

And in that space, freedom arises.

You are not the subtext. You are the awareness that sees beyond it.

Seeing the Footnotes of Your Life

Your experience of life may seem like a finished manuscript, its meaning already set in ink. But beneath the printed words, hidden notes shape the way you read the story—subtle influences that shape your thoughts, reactions, and sense of self. These are the unconscious beliefs you carry, inherited from the past, absorbed without question. They color how you see yourself, how you interpret the world, and how you move through life.

Most people are unaware of these footnotes. They read only the main text, believing that their experience of life is objective and real. But much of what you think, feel, and do is shaped by these invisible assumptions, written into your mind long before you ever had the awareness to question them.

How do you access these hidden footnotes?

» **Observe Your Emotional Reactions.** Every time you feel triggered, anxious, or defensive, there is a footnote beneath that reaction. Ask yourself: *What belief is operating here? What unspoken assumption is shaping my response?* Simply noticing creates space between you and the reaction.

» **Listen to the Mind Without Believing It.** The mind constantly narrates your life. Pay attention to this voice, but instead of assuming it is telling the truth, observe it like an outsider. When it says, *"I can't do this,"* ask: *Who is saying this? Where did this belief come from?*

» **Watch for Repeating Patterns.** If the same kinds of challenges, relationships, or struggles keep appearing in your life, they are pointing to an underlying belief. Life is not doing this to you—it is reflecting something within you. Ask: *What belief am I unconsciously living out?*

» **Sit in Stillness.** Beyond the movement of thought, there is a quiet presence within you. In stillness, the unconscious reveals itself not as a problem to be solved but as something to be seen. You do not need to force insights—simply being present allows them to arise.

The more you access the footnotes of your life, the less

power they have over you. What was once hidden is now seen. And what is seen loses its grip.

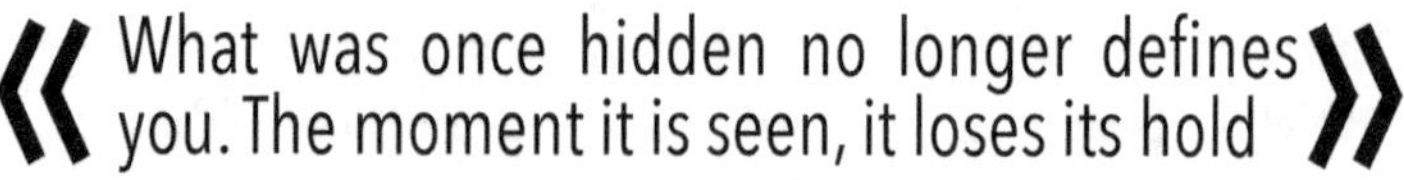

Awareness dissolves the grip of the unconscious. Yet, what remains unseen continues to shape our reality. Many have attempted to map the hidden layers of the mind, but few have explored its depths as profoundly as Carl Jung.

Case Study: Carl Jung – The Unconscious Mind and the Power of Self-Exploration

For centuries, the greatest minds have sought to understand the unconscious. Carl Jung, one of the most profound explorers of the unseen mind, revealed a deeper truth: much of what we do, think, and feel does not arise from conscious awareness—it comes from somewhere deeper.

Carl Jung devoted his life to exploring this hidden dimension of the mind. He saw that most people live unaware of the forces moving within them, mistaking conditioned patterns and inherited beliefs for their own thoughts. He understood that until we bring these unconscious aspects into awareness, they will continue to shape our lives, appearing as fate.

Jung did not view the unconscious as something to be feared or repressed. He saw it as a portal to self-discovery, a place where the truth of who we are waits to be seen. He called this process *individuation*—the journey of integrating what is hidden, dissolving illusions, and awakening to wholeness.

Exploring the Depths of the Mind

For Jung, the unconscious was not just a shadowy realm of forgotten memories and suppressed emotions. It was also the source of deep wisdom, creativity, and transformation. He saw that within each person, there is a tension between the ego—the part of us that clings to identity and control—and the deeper self, which seeks integration and awakening.

Rather than resisting the unconscious, Jung encouraged people to meet it with curiosity. He believed that by exploring our dreams, emotions, and recurring life patterns, we could begin to see the hidden forces that shape our experiences.

» **Observing the Shadow** – Jung called the unconscious aspects of ourselves the *shadow*. These are the parts we deny, repress, or project onto others. But the shadow is not the enemy—it is only the unseen. To integrate it, one must first see it.

» **Dialogue with the Unconscious** – Jung used a technique called *active imagination*, in which one allows unconscious images and emotions to surface, meeting them without resistance. He understood that when we listen without judgment, the unconscious reveals what needs to be known.

» **The Journey to Wholeness** – True self-exploration is not about fixing or improving oneself. It is about seeing through the illusion of separation, dissolving false identities, and realizing that the deeper self has always been present.

Awakening Through Awareness

Jung's greatest insight was that we do not need to fear the unconscious—we only need to bring awareness to it. What was once hidden loses its control over us when it is seen.

Your life, as it is now, is shaped by the stories and patterns of your unconscious mind. But the moment you become aware of them, they no longer define you. You realize that you are not the past, not the conditioning, not the fleeting thoughts that arise and fade.

You are the presence that sees.

And in that seeing, transformation begins.

The Free-Writing Exercise – Discovering Hidden Thoughts and Motivations

There is a voice inside your mind, always speaking, always narrating, always interpreting the world around you. But most of what it says goes unnoticed. You assume your thoughts are your own, that they are simply part of who you are. But in reality, many of them are conditioned patterns—unconscious beliefs inherited from the past.

Free-writing is a way to step outside of thinking to let the deeper layers of your mind reveal themselves without resistance. It is not about controlling your words or crafting a story. It is about observing what arises when the mind is given space to speak without censorship.

This is not an intellectual exercise. It is an act of presence— allowing thoughts to flow without interference, without judgment. What appears on the page is not good or bad, right or wrong. It is simply what has been waiting to be seen.

Step 1: Set the Space

Find a quiet place where you will not be interrupted. Take a deep breath. Feel the stillness of this moment. You are not trying to produce something. You are simply opening a door to the hidden layers of the mind.

Step 2: Begin Writing Without Thinking

Set a timer for 10 minutes. Pick up a pen or place your hands on the keyboard. Begin writing whatever comes. It does not need to make sense. Do not pause. Do not edit. If nothing comes, write: *I don't know what to write.* Write whatever is present, even if it is silence.

Step 3: Watch the Mind Without Judging

Notice the thoughts that arise as you write. The hesitation. The resistance. The impulse to correct or analyze. These are the mind's attempts to control the process. See them, but do not engage with them. Keep writing.

Step 4: Read with Awareness

When the timer ends, put the pen down. Breathe. Read what you have written, not as the author, but as the observer. Do not judge. Do not interpret. Simply notice. What patterns emerge? What words repeat? Is there emotion beneath the words? What does the mind reveal when it is not being controlled?

Step 5: Let It Go

You do not need to solve anything. You do not need to understand everything. The purpose of this exercise is not to force meaning but to bring awareness to what is already there.

The unconscious speaks when you stop trying to control it. Thoughts drift through awareness like clouds across the sky—appearing, shifting, then vanishing back into stillness. You are not the thoughts. You are the presence that sees them. And in that seeing, something deeper awakens.

•••

Hidden messages are woven throughout every book—and your mind is no different. What beliefs, patterns, or assumptions are shaping your decisions without your conscious awareness?

Each day, observe the thoughts that arise. Do they come from presence, or are they echoes of the past? See them. Do not resist them.

The moment you recognize them for what they are, they begin to lose their hold.

Chapter Eight

Interpreting Themes – Core Life Patterns

"Do the thing, and you shall have the power."
— Ralph Waldo Emerson

Recognizing the Patterns That Shape Your Life

Life is not as random as it appears. Beneath the surface of daily experiences, there are patterns—recurring themes that shape your journey. These patterns are not coincidences; they are reflections of the unconscious mind, repeating themselves until they are seen.

Perhaps you notice that certain struggles arise again and again, each time wearing a different mask. Relationships that end the same way. Opportunities that slip through your fingers. Feelings of doubt that return, no matter how much you achieve. Or maybe you see a pattern of success, moments when life flows effortlessly as if guiding you toward something greater.

These themes are not happening *to* you. They are happening *through* you. They are invitations to wake up—to see where you are still identified with the past, where old conditioning is shaping the present moment.

When you become aware of these patterns, something shifts. You are no longer trapped in the cycle, mistaking repetition for reality. You see it for what it is: an echo of the mind's conditioning.

And in that seeing, the pattern loses its grip.

You are not the story that keeps repeating. You are the awareness that sees it. And in that awareness, new possibilities emerge.

The Patterns Beneath the Patterns

Patterns do not exist in isolation. What repeats in your life is not just an external event but a deeper energetic imprint— one shaped by past conditioning, replaying itself until it is seen. The same disappointments, the same struggles, the same emotional highs and lows—these are not random occurrences. They are manifestations of unresolved inner experiences.

If you look closely, you will see that these themes are not about what is happening *outside* of you but about what is being carried *within* you. A cycle of failed relationships may not be about others—it may be a reflection of unexamined fears of abandonment or the mind's attachment to an identity built around struggle. A pattern of success followed by self-sabotage may not be about external circumstances—it may be the result of an unconscious belief that you are undeserving or that happiness cannot last.

The mind clings to familiar emotional experiences, even

when they cause suffering. Why? Because to the mind, the known is safer than the unknown. If struggle has always been a part of your story, the mind may unconsciously recreate it, mistaking struggle for identity. If validation has always been chased, the mind may continue searching for it, believing that without approval, there is nothing.

But the moment you bring awareness to these patterns, you step outside of them. You see that they are not *who you are*, only conditioned responses playing themselves out. You do not need to resist them, fix them, or fight them. You only need to see them clearly.

❮❮ These patterns are not happening to you. They are happening through you. ❯❯

What you seen clearly no longer owns you. The moment it is brought into awareness, its power fades. And in that space, something new emerges—not from past identity, but from the freedom of presence.

From Awareness to Action: The Power of Growth

When you become aware of the patterns in your life, you realize that they are neither good nor bad. They are simply reflections of what has been unconscious. But what happens when awareness turns into conscious action? When instead of being ruled by conditioned responses, you choose to engage fully with the present moment?

Some patterns arise from fear, from avoidance, from the need to be seen in a certain way. But other patterns—when rooted in deep presence—become the foundation for true mastery. This is the difference between unconscious striving and conscious growth. It is not about chasing an idea of success. It is about being fully present in the process itself.

Yet awareness does not only dissolve struggle—it also reveals a path to mastery. The same patterns that once created limitation can become pathways to growth when met with presence. Kobe Bryant understood this deeply. He did not seek to change the game—he sought to fully engage with it, not by chasing success but by surrendering to the process itself.

Case Study: Kobe Bryant – The Presence of Relentless Growth

Kobe Bryant was known for his talent, but it was not talent that defined him. It was presence—the unwavering attention he brought to every moment of his craft. To many, he was obsessive, training while others rested. He studied the game when others celebrated. But his true gift was not just skill or work ethic—it was his ability to be completely engaged with whatever he was doing.

This is what made him different.

For Kobe, improvement was not something that happened later—it was always happening *now*. Every shot, every failure, every practice was an opportunity to grow. He did not see mistakes as setbacks. He saw them as feedback, as guides leading him deeper into mastery.

But what was driving him? Was it the pursuit of greatness? Was it the need to prove something? No. His success did not come from chasing an outcome. It came from his willingness to surrender to the process itself.

The Path of Conscious Mastery

» **Relentless Presence** - Kobe was not thinking about

future championships while he practiced. He was simply *there*, fully immersed in the repetition, in the movement, in the learning.

» **Discomfort as a Teacher:** He did not resist struggle. He leaned into it. He understood that discomfort is not an obstacle—it is an opening, a space where growth happens.

» **Ego as an Illusion:** He did not let failure define him. He did not cling to success. He saw both as temporary. What mattered was the *work itself.*

Kobe Bryant's greatness was not a result of external success. It was a result of deep inner discipline—the ability to fully engage in the present, to commit completely, not to an outcome, but to the process of growth itself.

This is the shift. When you are no longer seeking success but simply showing up fully present with what you are doing, mastery arises. Not from effort but from surrender. Not from forcing but from being.

True greatness is not about what you achieve; it is about who you are while you are doing it.

The Reframing Exercise – Transforming Negative Themes into Powerful Growth Narratives

There are stories running through your mind, shaping the way you see yourself and the world. These stories feel real because they have been repeated so many times. But they are not reality. They are interpretations—mental labels placed upon past experiences.

Perhaps you see yourself as someone who always fails. Or someone who is never chosen. Or someone who is not good enough. These are not facts. They are narratives constructed by the mind and reinforced by emotion.

But what happens when you step outside of the story? What happens when you see it not as who you are but simply as a thought arising in awareness?

Reframing is not about replacing one thought with another. It is about *seeing through* the illusion of the old story, recognizing that it is not truth—it is just one way of interpreting events. And once you see this, another perspective becomes available. A perspective rooted not in past conditioning but in presence.

Step 1: Identify the Story You've Been Telling Yourself

Write down one belief that keeps repeating in your life. Something the mind tells you about yourself.

Examples:

> » *"I always fail."*

> » *"I am not lovable."*

> » *"I will never be successful."*

Pause. Read what you have written. Notice how the mind wants to justify it, to collect proof from the past. But ask yourself: *Is this belief an absolute truth? Or is it simply a thought?*

Step 2: Observe the Story Without Identifying With It

For a moment, let go of the belief. Imagine watching it from a distance as if it were a cloud passing in the sky.

Ask yourself:

> » *Where did this story come from?*

> » *Is it happening now, or is it just a memory?*

> » *Who would I be without this thought?*

There is a space between you and the belief. This space is presence. And in this space, the old story begins to lose its grip.

Step 3: Shift from Story to Growth

Now, instead of trying to replace the belief with a forced positive affirmation, look for the deeper truth within your experience. Every challenge, every perceived failure, every struggle has offered something.

Ask:

> » *What has this experience taught me?*

> » *How has it strengthened me?*

> » *What if this was never a failure but a lesson leading me somewhere greater?*

Rewrite your narrative—not from the mind's need to control but from the clarity of awareness.

Examples:

> » *"I always fail." — "Every challenge has made me more resilient. Each time, I have learned something new."*

> » *"I am not lovable." — "Love is not something to be earned. It is something to be recognized within myself."*

> » *"I will never be successful." — "Success is not a destination. It is the presence I bring to this moment."*

Step 4: Live From This New Awareness

This is not about forcing a new belief. It is about stepping out of identification with the old one. Every time the mind tries to repeat the old story, simply notice it. See it as a thought, not as reality. And in that seeing, you will find freedom.

Because you are not the story. You are the awareness in which all stories arise and dissolve. And in presence, a new path unfolds—not from the past, but from the limitless possibility of now.

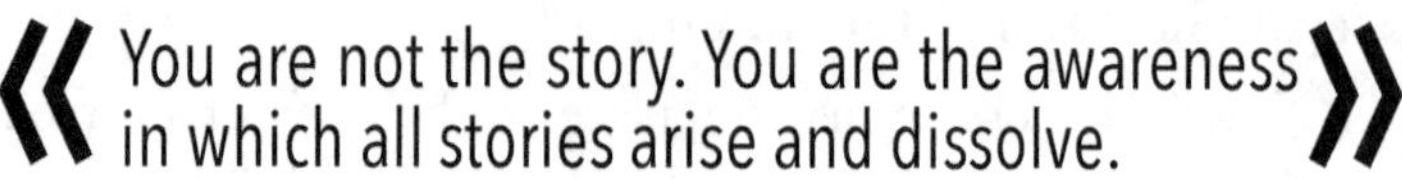

•••

Patterns appear, but they do not define you. The storyteller is not the story. Do not try to change the pattern—simply see it.

In that stillness, transformation happens—not through effort but through presence itself.

Chapter Nine

The Protagonist's Journey – Embracing Growth and Change

"The cave you fear to enter holds the treasure you seek."

—Joseph Campbell

Where Are You in Your Own Story?

Life unfolds like a story, but unlike a book, its meaning is not fixed. You are not merely a character following a script—you are also the awareness in which the story appears. The mind tries to place you somewhere in a personal narrative, assigning roles and labeling events as beginnings or endings. But where are you, truly?

Perhaps you feel as if you are at the start of something new, filled with uncertainty. Or maybe you are in the middle of a struggle, believing that resolution lies somewhere ahead. You may even sense that a chapter is closing, that something is shifting, yet you do not know what comes next.

The mind wants to define where you are—*I am stuck. I am behind. I am lost.* But these are only thoughts, conditioned interpretations of the present moment. In reality, there is no fixed arc, no predetermined path. There is only now.

Where you are in your personal story is not determined by external events but by your level of presence. Are you here, or are you caught in resistance, in longing, in trying to reach the next chapter?

The story changes when you stop searching for your place within it. You do not need to force growth or control change. Growth happens on its own when you step fully into this moment. Change is not something to resist or chase—it is simply life moving as it always has.

You are not the story. You are the awareness in which it unfolds. And in that awareness, you are always exactly where you need to be.

The Hero's Journey as a Metaphor for Awakening

The journey of self-growth is often imagined as a path toward becoming something greater, a process of overcoming obstacles, achieving success, or finding deeper meaning. But in reality, it is not about *becoming* anything—it is about *remembering* who you have always been.

Joseph Campbell's *The Hero's Journey* describes a universal pattern: a call to adventure, challenges that force transformation, and a return home, forever changed. This is not just a mythological structure—it is a reflection of human experience, the unfolding of consciousness itself.

《 Growth does not happen in the known. It happens when you step into the unknown– not to find something, but to surrender to what is already here **》**

At some point, life presents you with a challenge, an invitation to step beyond the familiar. The mind resists—it prefers comfort, certainty, the illusion of control. But growth does not happen in the known. It happens when you step into the unknown, not in search of something outside of yourself, but in surrender to what is already here.

There will be struggles. Not because life is against you but because the mind clings to old patterns, fearing what lies beyond them. But struggle is not the enemy. It is the fire that dissolves false identities, revealing the deeper awareness beneath them.

Eventually, the journey leads you back to yourself. But you are not the same. Or rather, you are—but now you *see*. You return to the same world, yet everything is different because you no longer look at it through the lens of resistance. You no longer search for meaning—you simply *are*.

The true hero's journey is not about reaching a destination. It is about awakening to the present moment again and again. And in that awareness, you realize—there was never anything missing. You were home all along.

From Struggle to Awareness: The Hidden Gift of the Journey

The Hero's Journey is not about escaping struggle. It is about seeing struggle for what it is—not as an obstacle, but as a doorway. Pain is not a barrier to growth; it is part of the journey itself. The search for meaning in the future is an illusion—meaning is not found in escaping hardship but in meeting it fully in this moment.

When you stop resisting hardship, something shifts. You see that suffering does not diminish you—it strips away illusion. It forces you to let go of what is temporary and brings you face-to-face with what is real. True transformation does not happen when suffering ends. It happens when you stop identifying with it.

Few have understood this more deeply than Viktor Frankl. In one of the darkest places imaginable, he did not resist suffering—he met it with presence. In doing so, he discovered a truth that would transform not only his own life but the lives of many others.

Case Study: Viktor Frankl - Meaning Beyond Suffering

Viktor Frankl endured one of the darkest experiences imaginable—imprisonment in a Nazi concentration camp. Everything external was taken from him—his home, his family, his freedom. Yet, in the midst of unimaginable suffering, he discovered something that could never be taken: his inner freedom.

At first, like everyone around him, he felt despair. The mind tells a story—*This is unfair. This is unbearable. This is the end.* But something in him remained awake, watching. He saw that those who survived were not necessarily the strongest nor the ones who fought hardest against their suffering. They were the ones who found meaning in it.

Frankl realized that even in suffering, a person can choose

how to respond. He saw that the moment suffering is given meaning, it is no longer suffering—it becomes transformation.

Presence in the Face of Darkness

» **Freedom Within:** Though physically imprisoned, Frankl understood that his mind—his inner state—was his own. No external force could take that from him.

» **Meaning as Survival:** He observed that those who found a purpose—whether it was the hope of reuniting with loved ones or the belief that their suffering had meaning—were far more likely to survive than those who surrendered to despair.

» **Detachment from Pain:** He learned that pain was real, but identification with it was a choice. He could either let it define him, or he could witness it from a place of presence.

Frankl wrote that *"Everything can be taken from a person except one thing—the last of human freedoms: to choose one's attitude in any given set of circumstances, to choose one's own way."*

His suffering did not make him weaker. It did not break him. It awakened him. He saw that meaning is not found in avoiding pain but in meeting it fully, without resistance.

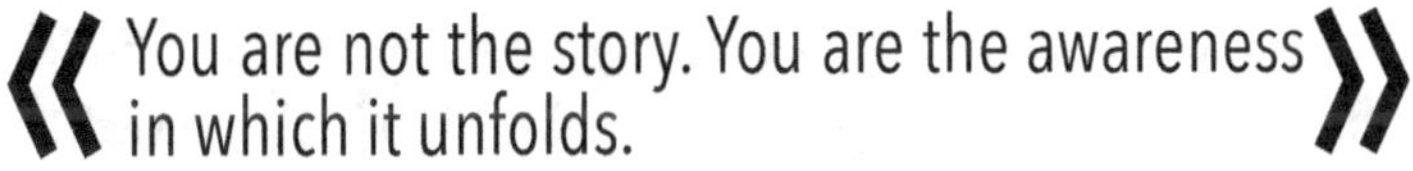

The Shift: Seeing Suffering as a Pathway to Awareness

The Hero's Journey is not about escaping struggle. It is about recognizing struggle as part of the path itself. The mind resists pain, believing that meaning is found somewhere beyond suffering, somewhere in the future where all challenges have disappeared. But meaning is never in the future. It is always here.

No experience, no matter how painful, has the power to define you. Only your identification with it does. When suffering is seen as just another moment passing through awareness, its hold on you fades.

This is the shift. You are not what happens to you. You are the presence that sees it. And in that presence, meaning is already here.

The Turning Point Exercise – Seeing Struggle as Transformation

The mind believes struggle is something to avoid, something that blocks the path forward. It tells a story: *This shouldn't be happening. This is unfair. This is too much to bear.* But what if struggle is not in the way? What if it is the way?

Suffering does not exist to punish you. It exists to awaken you. Every difficulty, every disappointment, every loss is not an ending—it is a turning point. Not because life is forcing you to change but because it is inviting you to see. The moment suffering is met with awareness, it loses its grip. It no longer defines you—it transforms you.

This exercise is not about forcing yourself to be grateful for pain. It is about shifting your relationship with it. Not resisting. Not labeling it as wrong. Simply allowing it to be seen for what it is—an essential part of your journey.

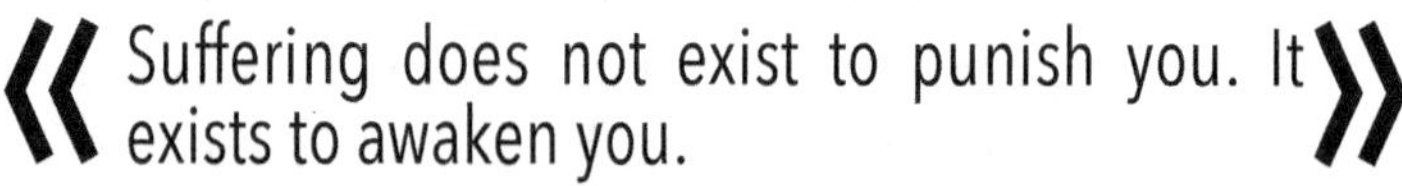

Step 1: Identify a Struggle That Has Defined You

Think of a difficult experience in your life. Something that felt unfair, painful, or overwhelming.

Write it down in a single sentence.

Examples:

> » *I was rejected from an opportunity I deeply wanted.*
>
> » *A relationship I invested in fell apart.*
>
> » *I have struggled with self-doubt for as long as I can remember.*

Pause. Read what you have written. Notice how the mind immediately begins to tell a story about it—*why it happened, what it means about you, what should have been different.* See the story, but do not engage with it.

Step 2: Shift from Resistance to Awareness

Now, ask yourself:

> » *Is this experience still happening, or is it just a memory?*
>
> » *Who would I be without the story I've attached to it?*
>
> » *Has this struggle shown me something I would not have seen otherwise?*

Let go of the mind's need to explain, justify, or analyze. Simply sit with these questions. There is no right answer—there is only presence.

Step 3: Find the Turning Point

Instead of asking *Why did this happen to me?*, ask:

> » *How has this shaped me?*
>
> » *What did this force me to let go of?*
>
> » *What strength, wisdom, or clarity has emerged because of this?*

Write down one sentence that shifts your perspective.

Examples:

» *That rejection led me to a path I never would have chosen—but one that ultimately fulfilled me.*

» *Losing that relationship freed me from an identity I had outgrown.*

» *My struggle with self-doubt has taught me the difference between my thoughts and who I truly am.*

This is the turning point—not in the story itself, but in how you see it.

Step 4: Release the Story

You do not need to force meaning onto suffering. You do not need to reframe pain into something positive. Simply recognize that it no longer owns you.

Every time the mind tries to return to this struggle, notice it. Do not resist it. Just observe: *There is that story again.*

And then return to presence. The struggle has already done what it was meant to do. It has awakened something in you. That is enough.

Because you are not the struggle. You are the awareness in which struggle arises and dissolves. And in that awareness, you are already free.

• • •

Every protagonist faces challenges, but they also grow because of them. You are no different. Where are you in your own hero's journey?

Do not rush to change or fix anything—simply see it. And in that seeing, the next step will reveal itself.

PART THREE

Editing and Rewriting Your Story

*"The privilege of a lifetime is to become who
you truly are."*

— Carl Jung

Every book goes through an editing process before it's complete. The same is true for personal transformation. Now that you've explored the chapters of your life and uncovered the deeper themes, it's time to take control of the story.

This section will guide you through the process of revision—rewriting outdated beliefs, adjusting your internal dialogue, and embracing a new, more authentic narrative. You are both the author and the protagonist.

It's time to write the next chapter with intention.

We'd Love to Hear From You!

Thank you so much for reading this book-it means the world to me. If you found it helpful, inspiring, or just enjoyable, would you take a moment to leave a review? Your feedback not only helps others but also keeps me motivated to create more valuable content for you.

Here's how you can leave a review:

1. Scan the QR code on this page to go directly to the author's page.

2. Or, visit your Amazon Orders page, find this book, and click "Write a Product Review."

Your kind words make a big difference.
Thank you for your support!

Chapter Ten

Revising Your Story - Rewriting Your Life Script

"You can't go back and change the beginning, but you can start where you are and change the ending."

— C.S. Lewis

Becoming Your Own Editor: Rewriting the Narrative of Your Life

The mind tells a story about who you are. It collects memories, beliefs, and experiences, weaving them into an identity. *This is me. This is how life works. This is what I can or cannot do.* But what if this story is not truth? What if it is simply a script that has been written and rewritten so many times that you have forgotten you are the one holding the pen?

To become your own editor means to step back from the narrative and see it for what it is—just words, just thoughts.

The mind repeats familiar patterns, not because they are real, but because they are known. You may believe *I am not good enough,* or *I always fail because these thoughts have played on a loop for so long that they feel like reality.* But they are not reality. They are just conditioned beliefs passed down from the past.

An editor does not accept every word as final. An editor questions, revises, and removes what no longer serves the story. You can do the same.

> » Challenge the beliefs that limit you. Ask: *Is this absolutely true? Or is it just something I have believed without question?*

> » Observe the patterns in your thinking. Do certain thoughts repeat like a script? Are they based on presence, or are they echoes of the past?

> » Let go of old narratives. Just because a story has been told does not mean it must continue. The moment you see it for what it is, you are no longer bound by it.

You are not the character in the story. You are the awareness in which the story arises and dissolves. And in that awareness, a new script can unfold—not from effort but from freedom.

Reframing the Mind's Story: Shifting from Illusion to Awareness

The mind tells a story about your life. It labels experiences as good or bad, success or failure. It clings to the past and projects onto the future, believing that who you are is defined by what has happened to you.

But these are only thoughts—interpretations, not reality.

Cognitive reframing is not about replacing one thought

with another. It is about seeing through the illusion of thought itself. The mind creates meaning out of events, but that meaning is not fixed. It is not truth. It is simply a perspective, one that can shift the moment you bring awareness to it.

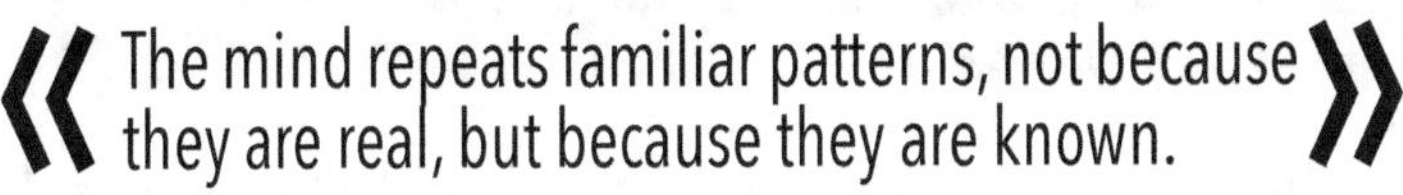

Techniques for Reframing Your Story

Question the Thought

A thought arises: *I always fail.* The mind accepts it as truth. But is it?

Ask yourself:

> » *Is this absolutely true?*

> » *Am I seeing the full picture, or only what confirms my belief?*

> » *Who would I be without this thought?*

The moment you question a thought, you create space between you and the thought. And in that space, freedom arises.

See the Lesson, Not the Loss

The mind resists struggle, believing that suffering is meaningless. But awareness sees something deeper. Every challenge, every setback, every painful experience carries something beneath it—not as a lesson forced upon you, but as an opportunity for awakening.

Instead of asking, *Why did this happen to me?*

Ask:

> » *What strength has this revealed in me?*

> » *How has this experience helped me to let go of what no longer serves me?*

> » *What if this was never a failure but a step toward something greater?*

The past cannot define you. Only your identification with it does.

Shift from Victim to Observer

The mind creates stories of blame: *This person hurt me. This situation ruined me. This should not have happened.*

But what if you are not the victim of the story? What if you are simply the awareness watching it unfold?

Instead of identifying with the pain, step back.

Observe:

> » *This is a thought. This is an emotion. This is a memory.*

> » *But I am not the thought. I am not the emotion. I am the presence in which they appear and dissolve.*

When you step into awareness, suffering loses its hold. The story shifts—not by force, but by seeing.

The Power of Presence in Reframing

Cognitive reframing is not about forcing positivity. It is about waking up. It is about recognizing that no thought, no story, no past event can define you unless you cling to it.

Let the story unfold. Let thoughts arise and dissolve. But know that who you are is not the story—who you are is the awareness that sees it.

And in that seeing, the story no longer controls you. It simply flows.

From Thought to Presence: Seeing Beyond the Story

Reframing is not about changing a thought—it is about recognizing that thoughts do not define you. You are the presence that sees them come and go. The moment you recognize a belief as just a thought, it begins to lose its power over you. Instead of being trapped in an old narrative, you become aware of something deeper.

Some people glimpse this truth and consciously rewrite the way they see their lives. But what happens when someone not only shifts their perception but also changes what unfolds around them?

Few have demonstrated this more powerfully than Jim Carrey. His story reveals that the greatest shifts happen not by forcing change but by stepping fully into the present moment—where transformation is already unfolding.

Case Study: Jim Carrey – The $10 Million Check and the Power of Awareness

Before Jim Carrey was a household name, before the world saw him as the comedian and actor he became, he saw himself in a different way. He was struggling, unknown, and nearly broke. But one moment changed the way he saw reality—not because his circumstances shifted, but because his perception did.

One night, sitting in his car overlooking Los Angeles, Carrey made a decision. He wrote himself a check for $10 million for "acting services rendered," postdated it for five years in the future, and kept it in his wallet. Every day, he saw it.

Every day, he reminded himself of not just what he wanted but who he already was.

The mind would say, *This is just a dream. This is unrealistic.* But Carrey did not dwell on doubt. He did not cling to the thought, *One day, I will be successful.* He lived as if it was already unfolding—not through force, but through certainty. He let go of resistance.

And what happened? Almost exactly five years later, he was cast in *Dumb and Dumber*—earning, astonishingly, a $10 million paycheck.

The Deeper Truth: Visualization as an Act of Presence

This is not about magical thinking. It is not about wishing for something and hoping it appears. It is about alignment with reality as it is—not as the mind perceives it.

Carrey did not sit idly, hoping his vision would manifest. He did not chase it with desperation. Instead, he stepped into the reality of what was already present. He acted, lived, and moved through the world as if his story had already changed—not because he was forcing an outcome, but because he no longer identified with lack.

What made the difference?

> » He saw himself beyond his circumstances. He did not let struggle define him.

> » He let go of doubt. He did not resist where he was—he simply kept moving toward what was already unfolding.

> » He stayed in the present. He did not obsess over how or when things would happen. He remained in alignment with the belief that it was already real.

Rewriting Your Own Reality

Jim Carrey's story is not about the check. It is about detachment from the old script and stepping into something new.

The mind clings to identity—*This is who I am. This is how life works.* But what if you could see through that? What if your reality is only limited by the story you keep telling yourself?

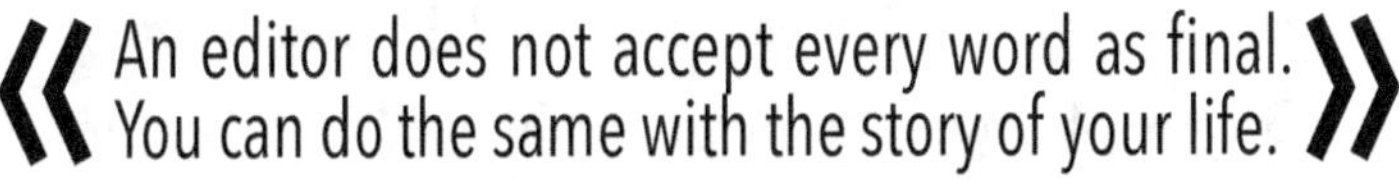

True visualization is not about wishing for something to happen. It is about realizing that you are not separate from it. You are already the awareness in which it exists.

When you stop clinging to the past and stop resisting the present, the story shifts—not by effort, but by surrender.

Because you are not the story. You are the presence in which all stories arise and dissolve.

From Story to Presence: Letting Go of the Old Script

The mind clings to identity—it tells a story about who you are, what has happened to you, and what your life should be. It assigns meaning to events, labeling them as good or bad, success or failure. But these are just words, interpretations— not truth.

Some people reach a breaking point where the old story no longer works. A moment when everything they thought they knew about themselves collapses. But if they can see beyond the illusion of control, something deeper emerges—a space where transformation happens not by force but by surrender.

This was the journey of Elizabeth Gilbert.

Case Study: Elizabeth Gilbert – Rewriting Her Life After Divorce

Before she was the author of *Eat, Pray, Love*, before she became a voice of self-discovery and reinvention, Elizabeth Gilbert was lost in a life that no longer fit her. She had everything that was supposed to make her happy—a marriage, a home, stability—but something inside her was crumbling.

Divorce shattered the identity she had built. The mind would say, *This is failure. This is the end.* But instead of resisting, instead of forcing herself to return to a life that no longer felt true, Gilbert did something different. She let go of the old script.

She stepped into the unknown, not with a plan, but with a willingness to explore life beyond the conditioned expectations placed upon her. She traveled, she listened, she sat in silence. She surrendered to the experience rather than clinging to the past.

The Power of Letting Go

Gilbert's story is not about escape. It is not about running away. It is about meeting herself beyond the roles she had been playing.

She realized:

» Pain was not an ending but a beginning. She did not need to fear the collapse of the old story—she needed to trust what was unfolding.

» She was not defined by failure. Divorce was not a sign that she had done something wrong. It was an invitation to step into something new.

» Stillness reveals truth. By traveling, meditating, and embracing solitude, she met herself beyond thought, beyond labels, and beyond expectations.

Her journey was not about finding happiness in another place. It was about awakening to the truth that happiness was never outside of her—it was always within.

Rewriting Your Own Story

Gilbert did not force a new narrative. She surrendered to the natural dissolution of the past. And in that space, something deeper could arise—not from striving, but from presence.

The mind tells a story: *I am lost. I don't know what's next.* But what if not knowing is not a problem? What if this moment, as it is, is exactly where transformation begins?

You do not need to force growth. You do not need to control the story. You only need to let go of what no longer serves you.

And in that surrender, a new path unfolds—not from the mind, but from the deeper intelligence of life itself.

The Rewrite Exercise - Seeing the Past Through Awareness

The mind clings to stories about the past. It replays old events, labeling them as *good* or *bad, success* or *failure.* It tells you what should have happened, what went wrong, and what it all means about you. But these are just thoughts—interpretations, not truth.

The past is not a fixed reality. It only exists as memory, a story the mind continues to tell. And like any story, it can be rewritten—not by changing what happened, but by shifting the perspective from which you see it.

This exercise is not about creating a false version of events. It is about stepping beyond the mind's conditioned narrative and seeing the deeper truth beneath the experience.

Step 1: Identify a Past Experience That Still Holds Power Over You

Think of a moment in your life that still lingers in your mind. Something that feels unresolved, something that shaped how you see yourself.

Write it down in one sentence, as the mind has been telling it.

Examples:

> » *I failed that opportunity, and it proved I wasn't good enough.*

> » *That person betrayed me, and I will never trust again.*

> » *I made the wrong choice, and now I am stuck.*

Pause. Read the sentence. Notice how the mind wants to hold onto this version of the story. See the emotions that arise. But also see that this is just a thought—a collection of words, not reality itself.

Step 2: Observe the Story Without Identifying With It

Now, step back from the story. Instead of being inside it, imagine you are an observer, watching it unfold as if it were a scene in a movie.

Ask yourself:

> » *Is this story still happening, or is it just a memory?*

> » *Who would I be without this interpretation?*

> » *What if this event was not an ending but part of a larger*

unfolding?

Notice how the mind wants to justify the old narrative. It looks for proof, for reasons to hold onto the pain. But awareness does not need proof. Awareness simply sees.

Step 3: Rewrite the Story From Presence

Instead of writing from the mind's old perspective, rewrite the experience from a place of clarity and empowerment, not by changing the facts but by shifting the meaning.

Examples:

> » *That opportunity didn't work out, but it led me to something more aligned with who I truly am.*

> » *That betrayal taught me the difference between attachment and true connection.*

> » *The choice I made was the only choice I could have made in that moment, and I am still evolving.*

Feel the difference. The past has not changed, but your relationship with it has.

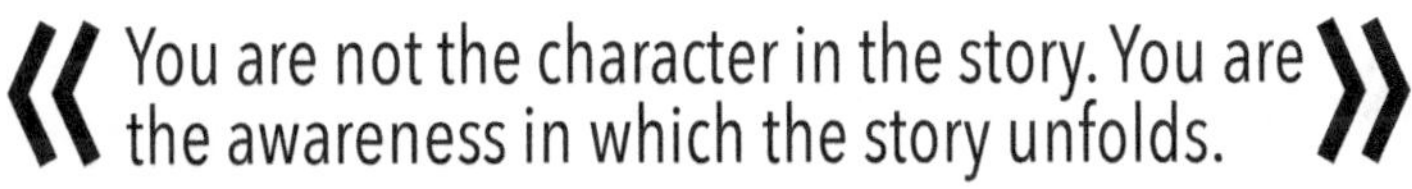

Step 4: Release the Story

Read both versions—the mind's old narrative and your new perspective. Which one feels lighter? Which one feels more aligned with the truth of who you are?

You do not need to force yourself to believe the new version. Simply notice that the story is not fixed—it is fluid. And in that recognition, you are free.

The past no longer owns you. The moment you see it with awareness, it loses its grip. Because you are not the story. You are the presence in which all stories arise and dissolve

...

Your story is not set in stone. Every great author revises their work, and you have that same power.

Chapter Eleven

Navigating Resistance – Rewriting Your Life Despite Pushback

"If you argue for your limitations, you get to keep them."

— Richard Bach

Why Resistance Happens

Change is unsettling—not just for you, but for those around you.

The mind craves familiarity. It seeks patterns, predictability, the comfort of what is known. When you evolve, when you begin to shift in ways that no longer fit the old structure, resistance arises. Not because something is wrong but because something is different.

People become attached to their version of who you are. They know you as predictable, as someone who plays a familiar role in their story. Your transformation, then, does not just challenge your past—it challenges their perception of reality.

Resistance is rarely personal. It is not truly about you. It is the mind's way of holding onto what feels safe.

>> Resistance is not a sign to stop–it is a sign that you are moving beyond where you once were. <<

The Illusion of Stability

The mind believes that stability comes from keeping things the same. It tells itself, *If nothing changes, I will be secure.* This is an illusion. Nothing is permanent. Life is movement, unfolding moment by moment.

And yet, when you change—when you step beyond the old version of yourself—the people around you may react. Not because they wish to hold you back but because your transformation forces them to look at themselves.

They asks themselves:

> » *If he is growing, why am I staying the same?*

> » *If she is evolving, what does that mean for me?*

> » *Can I accept this change, or do I resist it to preserve my sense of self?*

Why People Resist the Growth of Others

Resistance arises not from malice but from fear. When you change, it forces others to confront their own limitations.

Fear of the Unknown – Your transformation disrupts their perception of reality. If you step into something new, it forces them to ask:

>> *Am I capable of change, too?*

The mind resists uncertainty, clinging to the familiar, even when the familiar no longer serves.

Loss of Control – Relationships form unspoken agreements. You behave in a certain way, they respond in a certain way. When you shift, you break that pattern. The mind reacts to this as a loss of control.

Threat to Identity – If someone has always known you as the quiet one, the fixer, the person who never says no, your transformation forces them to reexamine their own identity.

>> *If you are no longer playing your role, who am I in this relationship?*

Projection of Limitation – Sometimes, resistance is not about you at all. It is about their own beliefs. If someone has spent years believing that change is impossible, your growth contradicts that belief. It is easier for them to doubt you than to question themselves.

Recognizing Different Types of Resistance

Resistance does not always appear as open opposition. Sometimes, it is quiet—hidden in hesitation, masked as concern, disguised as logic.

The mind does not always say stop directly. Instead, it whispers:

>> *Are you sure?*

>> *What if this is a mistake?*

>> *What will others think?*

To move through resistance, you must first see it for what it is.

Family & Friends: Fear of Losing the "Old You"

People attach to the version of you they have always known. Your growth, then, is not just about you—it affects them as well.

> » *"Remember when you used to be fun?"* (Nostalgia as resistance.)

> » *"Are you sure this is the right choice?"* (Doubt disguised as concern.)

> » Quiet withdrawal when your change feels unfamiliar to them.

They do not resist because they do not care. They resist because your transformation disrupts the roles they are used to playing.

Workplace & Society: Professional Expectations and Social Labels

Culture, tradition, and expectations shape how the world sees you. When you begin to shift, society often urges you to return to the familiar.

> » *"Why are you trying something new?"* (Skepticism from colleagues.)

> » *"This is the way it's always been done."* (Pressure to conform.)

> » *"People like you don't do that."* (Cultural norms discouraging change.)

The world prefers what is predictable. When you step beyond the expected, you challenge not just a system but the collective belief in what is possible.

Internalized Resistance: When External Doubts Become Self-Doubt

Not all resistance comes from others. Some of it is within you—the echoes of past conditioning, the mind's attempt to keep you safe by keeping you small.

> » *"I'll change when I'm fully ready."* (Perfectionism masking procrastination.)

> » *"If I change too much, I won't belong anymore."* (Fear of standing out.)

The greatest resistance is often the one you do not recognize—your own hesitation to fully step into who you are becoming.

Seeing Resistance for What It Is

Resistance is not a barrier. It is a mirror. It reflects where attachment still exists, where identity still clings to old definitions.

Ask yourself:

> » *Am I hesitating because something is wrong or because something is unfamiliar?*

> » *Is this my fear, or am I carrying the fears of others?*

> » *If I moved forward without resistance, what would be possible?*

You do not need to fight resistance.

You only need to see through it.

Because when you no longer seek validation, there is nothing left to resist.

How to Navigate Pushback Without Losing Momentum

The mind seeks validation. It wants certainty, agreement, and reassurance that the path you are walking is the right one. But transformation is rarely met with universal approval. Growth, by its nature, disrupts. It shifts the roles that others have grown comfortable with.

When you change, some will support you. Others will question, doubt, or resist. The mistake is believing that their reaction is your barrier.

Pushback is not an obstacle. It is an invitation—to remain present, to trust yourself, and to move forward without needing external permission.

Setting Boundaries While Maintaining Relationships

A boundary is not a wall. It is not created out of resistance or rejection. It is clarity—knowing where you end and where others begin.

When you grow, some will try to pull you back—not always with ill intent, but out of their own discomfort. They may challenge your choices, test your resolve, or expect you to remain as you were.

A boundary is not something you argue for. It is something you embody.

You do not have to convince them. You do not have to explain. Simply stand in your truth:

>» *"I understand your concern, but this is the direction I*

choose."

> *"I hear you, but my path is my own."*

Others may resist, but their resistance is not yours to carry. You are not responsible for how others react to your evolution. You are only responsible for continuing to grow.

Responding to Criticism with Confidence and Clarity

Criticism is inevitable. Some will say you are changing too much; others will say you are not changing enough. The mind may be tempted to defend, to explain, to seek understanding.

But truth does not need defense.

Ask yourself:

> *Is this criticism revealing something I need to see, or is it simply fear disguised as advice?*

> *Am I responding from presence or from the need to prove myself?*

> *If I remained still, without reaction, would the truth change?*

Not every criticism requires a response. Some dissolve in silence. If words are needed, let them come from stillness, not reactivity:

> *"I respect your perspective, but I trust my path."*

> *"I hear your concerns, and I am moving forward anyway."*

The need for validation fuels resistance. In its absence, judgment loses its weight.

❮❮ A boundary is not something you argue for– it is something you embody. ❯❯

Knowing When to Engage and When to Let Go

Not every conversation needs to be had. Not every person will understand your journey.

Engage when:

> » There is openness, curiosity, and mutual respect.
> » The conversation expands awareness rather than fuels argument.
> » There is space for listening, not just reaction.

Walk away when:

> » The discussion repeats itself without resolution.
> » You feel the need to justify your truth.
> » The energy is heavy, depleting, or rooted in control.

Some doors do not need to be closed. They simply stop being walked through.

Moving Forward Without Resistance

Pushback will come. Doubt will arise. The world will test your certainty—not to stop you, but to reveal how deeply you trust yourself.

Ask yourself:

> » *Am I seeking approval or living in alignment?*
> » *If I needed no validation, would I still move forward?*
> » *Who am I beyond the opinions of others?*

Growth does not require permission.

You do not need to fight resistance. You only need to see through it.

Because once you stop seeking acceptance, there is nothing left to push against.

Case Study: Trevor Noah – Reshaping Identity Amidst Resistance

The mind clings to identity. It says *This is who I am. This is where I belong.* It seeks certainty, a defined place within the familiar. But what happens when the world refuses to give you a label that fits?

Resistance is not always direct. Sometimes, it is woven into the very structure of the world. It does not just question your growth—it questions your right to exist as you are.

Trevor Noah was born into resistance. His very existence defied the system he was born into. Apartheid South Africa was a world of strict racial categories, but Noah, the son of a Black mother and a white father, fit into none of them. By law, he was "illegal." He could not walk freely with his parents and could not belong in the way others could.

For many, such a reality would become an identity—a story of exclusion, limitation, and powerlessness. However, Noah did not allow the system to define him. Instead, he observed it, moved between it, and ultimately transcended it.

Challenging Expectations: Humor as a Tool for Transformation

Where others saw barriers, Noah saw contradictions. Where others saw separation, he saw absurdity.

He realized that race, culture, and identity were not fixed realities but constructs enforced by the mind. Rather than resisting through anger, he chose something else: humor.

Humor was not just survival. It was awareness in action. It allowed him to move between cultures, speak the languages of different groups, and expose the illusion of division itself. He did not fight the system directly—he made it visible. And in doing so, he rewrote the narrative.

Redefining Himself Despite Pushback

As Noah's career grew, resistance followed. Some questioned his right to speak on global issues as a South African. Others doubted his ability to host *The Daily Show*. Some resisted his humor because it exposed uncomfortable truths.

But Noah did not seek permission. He did not attempt to fit expectations.

He simply continued.

Speaking. Learning. Moving forward.

He understood what many do not—identity is not fixed. It is not something you are given but something you create.

Key Points: The Path of Least Resistance is Not Submission–It is Awareness

Trevor Noah's journey is not just about breaking free from a system. It is about something deeper—the realization that identity is not a prison unless you make it one.

The mind wants to hold onto definitions: *This is who I am. This is where I belong.* But in truth, you are not a label. You are not a category. You are presence, unfolding, beyond limitation.

Ask yourself:

» *What labels have I accepted without question?*

» *Am I resisting change, or am I resisting the loss of who I thought I was?*

>> *If identity is fluid, what am I beyond it?*

Not everyone will understand your transformation. Not everyone will accept it. But that is not your burden to carry.

Because you were never meant to fit into the world's definitions, you were meant to move beyond them.

❮❮ Rejection is not a stop sign–it is a mirror, reflecting where you are still attached to old ❯❯ identities.

The Rejection Resilience Exercise

Rejection is only painful when you believe it defines you.

The mind creates an identity and clings to it, seeking validation, approval, and belonging. When rejection comes, it feels like an attack—not just on a choice, but on *who you are.* The mind says *I am not wanted. I am not enough. I should stop trying.*

But what if rejection is not about you at all?

What if it is simply a reflection of someone else's fear, their conditioning, their inability to see beyond their own perspective? What if rejection is not a block on your path but a sign that you are stepping beyond the familiar?

Rejection only has power *if you* make it personal. When you no longer define yourself by how others respond, rejection ceases to be an obstacle. It becomes a passing experience— nothing more.

This exercise will help you shift your perspective on rejection and see that when others push back, it is not a signal to retreat—it is an invitation to deepen your presence and continue forward.

Step 1: Identify a Moment of Rejection

Think of a time when you tried to step into something new—when you set a boundary, made a choice, or pursued a path that others did not understand. Instead of support, you were met with doubt, criticism, or silence.

Write down the situation in a single sentence. Keep it simple.

Examples:

> » I told my family I was changing careers, and they questioned whether I was making a mistake.

> » I tried to set a boundary with a friend, and they became distant.

> » I expressed a new belief, and people dismissed it.

Pause for a moment. Notice any tension that arises as you recall this moment. Observe it, but do not engage with it.

Step 2: Separate the Reaction from Reality

Now, write down the exact words or actions of rejection you encountered. Be specific.

> » *"You're being selfish."*

> » *"That's never going to work."*

> » *"Why are you changing? You used to be different."*

Next, describe how you felt in response. Did you feel hurt, frustrated, or misunderstood? Did self-doubt creep in? Did the resistance make you question yourself?

There is no right or wrong here. Simply notice. Observe

the emotions as if they were passing clouds in the sky. They are not you. They are experiences moving through awareness.

Step 3: Reframe Rejection as Growth, Not Failure

The mind sees rejection as a sign to stop. But what if rejection is not a denial but a redirection?

Look at the situation again and reframe it from a place of presence:

> **Instead of:** *"They don't believe in me."*
> **Try:** *"My growth challenges their perception of me."*
> **Instead of:** *"I am losing people by changing."*
> **Try:** *"Those who resonate with the new me will stay. Others are making space for what aligns."*
> **Instead of:** *"Maybe they are right. Maybe I should stop."*
> **Try:** *"Their doubt is theirs. My path remains unchanged."*

Write your new perspective. Read it slowly. Feel the shift in perception.

Rejection is no longer an obstacle. It is simply a sign that you are moving beyond where you once were.

Step 4: See Rejection as an Interpretation, Not an Identity

Close your eyes for a moment. Breathe. Imagine yourself standing at the edge of a river. The water flows, carrying away the voices of doubt, the opinions, the judgments.

You are not in the river. You are standing on the bank, watching.

Nothing is stopping you.

Rejection is not a measure of your truth—it is merely

someone else's reaction to your change. It does not define your path unless you allow it to. It is not a reflection of who you are but an interpretation seen through the lens of another's fears, conditioning, or expectations.

The moment you detach from the need for external validation, rejection loses its power over you.

Exercise Reflection

Now, ask yourself:

> » *If I no longer measure myself by how others respond to my growth, what remains?*

> » *Without the weight of rejection, how would I move forward?*

> » *If rejection is just a passing experience, what is truly stopping me?*

Stillness. Freedom. Presence.

Move forward, not in reaction to rejection, but in awareness of its impermanence.

Because you were never rejected—you were simply awakening.

• • •

Resistance is often a sign that you're on the right path. Every great story has obstacles—the question is, will you let them define your journey, or will you rewrite how the story unfolds?

Chapter Twelve

Editing Your Inner Dialogue

"Be yourself; everyone else is already taken."

— Oscar Wilde

The Power of Inner Dialogue: How Self-Talk Shapes Your Reality

The mind is always speaking. A voice narrates your life, interpreting events, forming opinions, and assigning meaning. Most people are unaware of this voice because they have never stopped to listen. It runs in the background, shaping emotions, influencing decisions, and reinforcing old identities.

But what if this voice is not telling the truth?

Your inner dialogue—your self-talk—creates the lens through which you see yourself and the world. If it is filled with doubt, you will perceive obstacles. If it is filled with judgment, you will assume others are judging you. If it constantly reminds you of past failures, you will hesitate before taking action.

The words you say to yourself are not just thoughts. They are instructions, shaping your identity, reinforcing who you believe yourself to be.

The Impact of Self-Talk on Self-Esteem

Self-esteem is not built on external validation; it is constructed from within. The mind, conditioned by past experiences, repeats familiar narratives: *I'm not good enough. I always fail. I don't belong.* These thoughts feel real because they have been repeated for so long. But they are not truth—they are only conditioned patterns, echoes of the past.

Imagine a child learning to walk. If they fall and someone tells them, *You will never walk. You are not strong enough*; they may believe it. But the falling is not the problem; it is the belief that forms around it.

Most people's self-dialogue is not their own. It is shaped by past wounds, external opinions, and society's expectations. But self-esteem is not found in these external voices—it is found in the silence behind them. Step back. Observe the voice. Do not identify with it. In that moment, a shift occurs.

> » Instead of *I am not enough*, you begin to see: *This is just a thought. It is not who I am.*

> » Instead of *I always fail*, you recognize: *Every setback has been a lesson, not a definition of who I am.*

The mind clings to self-criticism, believing it leads to growth. But judgment does not transform you. Awareness does. Bring presence to your thoughts, and they lose their grip.

How Self-Talk Influences Behavior

Your thoughts shape your actions. Your actions shape your

experience. A person who constantly tells themselves, I can't do this, will hesitate before trying. A person who believes I am unworthy of love will unconsciously push others away. The mind is like a script, and if you are unaware of it, you will continue playing the same role.

But the script can be rewritten.

> When the mind says, *This is impossible, step back and ask, Is this true, or is this fear speaking?*

> When the voice repeats, *I am a failure, recognize, This is just a thought passing through awareness. I am not the thought.*

> When you notice self-criticism, shift your attention from the words to the space behind them—the stillness that has never been harmed by any thought.

You do not need to argue with the inner voice. You do not need to replace every negative thought with a positive affirmation. You only need to see that the voice is not who you are.

The moment you stop believing every thought that arises, you step into freedom. And in that space, new possibilities emerge—not from force, but from presence.

Recognizing Thought Patterns and Shifting Perspective

The mind is conditioned to repeat familiar patterns. Most people live in a mental loop—hearing the same self-judgments, the same doubts, and the same stories about who they are and what they can or cannot do. These repetitive thoughts may feel real, but they are only habits of the mind. The moment you step back and observe them rather than identify with them, their grip begins to loosen.

Watch your thoughts. Do they sound familiar?

> » *I can't do this.* (Self-doubt)
> » *What if I fail?* (Fear)
> » *I should have done better.* (Regret)
> » *I don't deserve happiness.* (Unworthiness)

These are not truth. They are only echoes of the past.

These thoughts do not define you. They are echoes of past conditioning, absorbed from external influences, repeated so often they seem like truth.

But a thought, no matter how often repeated, remains just that—a thought.

Stepping Back: Becoming the Observer

The first step to shifting your inner dialogue is awareness. Instead of automatically believing your thoughts, observe them with detachment. When a thought arises—*I'm not good enough*—pause. See it as an outsider would, watching it appear and dissolve like a passing cloud.

Ask yourself:

> » *Is this absolutely true?*
> » *Would I say this to a friend?*
> » *What if this is just a habit, not reality?*

The moment you witness your thoughts without identifying with them, their power begins to fade. This is not about forcing a new belief but about moving from unconscious reaction to conscious awareness. The space that remains is not empty—it is where a new, more intentional narrative can take shape.

Replacing the Old Script with a Constructive Narrative

You do not need to force positive thinking. You do not need to battle your thoughts.

Your inner dialogue is not something to silence. It is something to refine.

Instead of reacting to every thought, see that you can choose which narratives to engage with.

Instead of I always fail, recognize:

> » *Every challenge teaches me something.*

> » *Growth happens, even when I cannot see it.*

Instead of I'm not good enough, realize:

> » *Worth is not earned—it is inherent.*

> » *I do not need to prove myself to be enough.*

Instead of I should have done better, accept:

> » *The past cannot be changed.*

> » *But I can meet this moment fully—without carrying past burdens.*

You do not need to force belief. See through the old one. The mind clings to stories. But without identification, they lose power.

Every moment is a chance to rewrite the narrative.

Not by fighting thoughts.

But by seeing that you are not them.

You are the awareness in which they arise.

Case Study: Muhammad Ali – The Power of Self-Belief

Most people wait for external validation before believing in themselves. They need proof before they claim their worth. But true transformation begins when you step beyond conditioned doubt and embody self-belief—before the world reflects it back to you.

Few understood this better than Muhammad Ali. Long before he was recognized as "The Greatest," he declared it himself—not as arrogance, but as an inner truth he refused to doubt. His words were not mere affirmations; they were alignments with reality before reality had caught up.

Speaking Reality into Existence

Ali did not wait for victory to claim greatness. He spoke it before it was recognized because he understood that belief shapes action.

> » *"I am the greatest,"* he repeated—not after he won, but before.

> » *"It's not bragging if you can back it up,"* he said—not as a defense, but as a statement of certainty.

The mind, conditioned by fear, often says, *"I'll believe it when I see it."*

But Ali reversed this thinking: *"When I believe it, I will see it."*

Overcoming External Doubt

Ali did not grow up in a world that encouraged him to see himself as great. The external voices told a different story—one of limitations, expectations, and doubt. But he did not internalize them. Instead, he replaced them with his own narrative:

» Instead of absorbing fear, he projected confidence.

» Instead of waiting for approval, he declared his own worth.

» Instead of following the script handed to him, he wrote his own.

Self-talk can be a cage or a key. If left unchecked, it becomes a prison of limitation. But when used with awareness, it becomes a doorway to possibility.

Self-Talk as Embodiment, Not Performance

Ali's affirmations were not wishful thinking. He did not say "I am the greatest" to convince himself—he embodied it. The power was not in the words themselves but in the absolute certainty behind them.

Most people repeat affirmations without belief, hoping the words will create the feeling. But true self-belief does not come from empty repetition—it comes from knowing.

You are not your doubts. You are not the voice that says you are not enough.

Like Ali, you do not need to wait for external proof. You do not need to wait for the world to validate your worth. Speak it now—not as something you hope to become, but as something you already are.

The Internal Editor Exercise – Practicing Self-Talk Rewrites in Real-Time

The mind is constantly narrating your life. It speaks before you act, comments on your choices, and often repeats the same conditioned thoughts over and over. But have you ever stopped to question whether this voice is actually telling the truth?

Most people accept their inner dialogue as reality. I always mess up. I'm not good enough. I'll never succeed. These thoughts arise automatically, shaping perception and behavior before they are even examined. But they are not facts. They are only mental habits—stories repeated so often that they feel real.

This exercise will help you become the editor of your own mind. Instead of passively accepting negative self-talk, you will practice catching these thoughts in real time and rewriting them with clarity and awareness.

Step 1: Catch the First Draft

Throughout the day, notice the way you speak to yourself. Pay attention to the automatic thoughts that arise, especially in moments of challenge, hesitation, or self-doubt.

Common examples include:

» *"I can't do this."*

» *"I always fail."*

» *"I'll never be good enough."*

Do not try to change the thought yet. Simply write it down as it appears, like an unedited first draft.

Step 2: Pause and Observe

Now, take a moment to step back. Instead of reacting to the thought, observe it.

Ask yourself:

» *Is this absolutely true, or is it just an old script playing out?*

» *Would I say this to a friend?*

» *What if this thought is just a habit, not a reality?*

By questioning the thought instead of automatically believing it, you create space between yourself and the conditioned mind. In this space, you are no longer trapped by the old narrative. You are the awareness watching it unfold.

Step 3: Rewrite the Thought with Awareness

Now, edit the script. This is not about replacing a negative thought with forced positivity. It is about shifting to a perspective that is both truthful and constructive.

Examples:

> **Original Thought:** *"I can't do this."*
> **Rewritten Thought:** *"I may not have done this before, but I am learning. Every step is progress."*
> **Original Thought:** *"I always fail."*
> **Rewritten Thought:** *"Failure is not an identity. Each experience teaches me something new."*
> **Original Thought:** *"I'm not good enough."*
> **Rewritten Thought:** *"My worth is not something to be earned. I do not need to prove myself to be enough."*

Notice that the rewrite is not blind optimism—it is a shift in perception. Instead of fighting the thought, you are stepping outside of it and seeing a deeper truth.

Step 4: Anchor the New Perspective in Presence

Once you have rewritten the thought, read it slowly. Feel the shift in energy. This is not just about changing words—it is about recognizing that you are not the mind's commentary. You are the awareness in which thoughts arise and dissolve.

Breathe deeply. Place your attention on the present moment.

Ask yourself:

> » *Without this old thought, who am I?*

> » *If I did not believe this limitation, what would be possible?*

There is no need to force a belief—only to see through the old one. The more you practice this, the less grip the conditioned mind has over you. And in that freedom, a new script begins to write itself—not from fear, but from clarity.

• • •

The words you speak to yourself create the reality you live in. Your inner dialogue can be rewritten just like any story.

What is one phrase you often tell yourself that diminishes your potential? Replace it with a new, empowering affirmation—and commit to saying it daily.

Chapter Thirteen

Publishing Your Authentic Self

"You either walk inside your story and own it, or you stand outside your story and hustle for your worthiness."

— Brené Brown

Embracing Your True Self and Aligning with Your Values

Who are you when there is no one to impress?

The world teaches you to play roles, to present versions of yourself that fit expectations. From an early age, you learn what is praised and what is rejected. You shape yourself accordingly, adapting to the approval of others, wearing masks that feel safe yet distant from something deeper.

But beneath these roles, something remains untouched.

Your true self—not the story, not the identity shaped by past conditioning, but the presence that is always here.

To embrace your true self is not to become something new but to recognize what has always been. It is not about adding, fixing, or perfecting—it is about removing what is false.

You do not need permission to be yourself.

You do not need validation to align with what feels true. The mind may ask, *What if I am judged? What if I do not belong?*

But belonging at the cost of authenticity is not belonging at all. It is performance.

When you align with your values, there is no conflict between what you feel inside and what you express in the world. There is no need to prove or defend. Truth does not argue—it simply is.

Ask yourself:

> » *Where am I still seeking approval?*
>
> » *Am I making choices from fear or from truth?*
>
> » *If I did not worry about rejection, how would I show up in the world?*

Your authentic self does not need to be created. It only needs to be uncovered. And when you step into it fully, there is no effort, only alignment.

No resistance, only flow.

No fear, only presence.

《 Authenticity is not something you achieve–it is what remains when you stop pretending. 》

Overcoming Fear of Judgment and Self-Doubt

Fear of judgment is the weight that keeps you small. It whispers, *What will they think? What if I fail? What if I am not enough?*

But who is this "they"?

And what is this "I" that seeks approval?

The mind creates an image of itself and then fears that this image will be criticized, rejected, or misunderstood. It searches for reassurance, for permission to exist without question. But the truth is, judgment comes and goes, like passing weather. It is only powerful if you hold onto it.

Self-doubt is not who you are. It is only a thought, a voice conditioned by past experiences. You were not born doubting yourself. You were not born afraid of being seen. These fears were learned. And anything learned can be unlearned.

When you live in fear of judgment, you imprison yourself within the opinions of others. You shrink, you hesitate, you censor your truth.

Ask yourself:

> » *Whose approval am I waiting for?*
>
> » *If no one else's opinion mattered, what would I do differently?*
>
> » *Who am I beyond the thoughts of self-doubt?*

You do not need to silence the fear. You only need to see through it. To observe it rather than become it.

If a child stumbles while learning to walk, does it stop trying because others might judge? No. The doubt is not natural—it is acquired. And just as it was acquired, it can be released.

You will never control how others perceive you. But you can be free from needing them to understand. The moment you stop living as a reflection of their opinions, you step into something greater: yourself, untouched by judgment, whole without validation.

Self-doubt does not dissolve when others approve of you. It dissolves when you no longer need them to. In presence, there is nothing to fear—only the space to be.

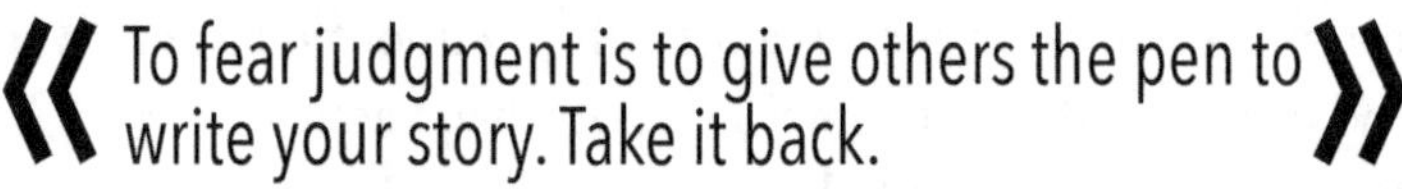

Case Study: Brené Brown – Vulnerability as Strength and the Power of Authenticity

Fear of judgment keeps many from showing up fully in their lives. The mind believes that to be seen is to be exposed, that to be vulnerable is to be weak. But awareness reveals something deeper: vulnerability is not weakness—it is presence, unguarded and real.

For years, Brené Brown studied vulnerability from a distance, as an academic researching human connection. She gathered data, analyzed patterns, and searched for understanding. But there was a moment—a breaking open—when she realized that vulnerability was not just a concept to study. It was something to be lived.

The story she had told herself was that control kept her safe. That perfection protected her. That if she could armor herself with certainty, she could avoid pain. But the truth she uncovered was this: growth does not come from protecting oneself. It comes from allowing oneself to be seen.

The Power of Vulnerability

» **Reframing Exposure** – What she had once feared—being emotionally exposed—became her greatest strength. She realized that connection is not built on invulnerability but on the courage to be real.

» **Letting Go of the Armor** – The perfectionism, the need to control, the fear of what others might think—these were not shields. They were walls, keeping her separate.

» **Transforming Fear into Freedom** – The willingness to be vulnerable—to stand in uncertainty, to risk failure, to be seen without pretense—became the foundation of her work.

Through research, storytelling, and lived experience, Brené Brown showed that vulnerability is not a liability—it is the birthplace of authenticity, courage, and love.

She did not conquer fear. She made space for it, saw through it, and in that seeing, was no longer bound by it.

Key Points: You do not need to be perfect to be worthy. You do not need to be certain to move forward. Vulnerability is not something to overcome—it is something to embrace.

Case Study: Maya Angelou – Self-Reinvention and Embracing Personal Power

Who you have been is not who you must become.

The mind clings to identity—to the roles it has played, to the expectations it has accepted. It says, *This is who I am, and I cannot change.* But awareness dissolves the illusion of fixed identity. The self is not static. It is fluid, expansive, and uncontained.

Maya Angelou embodied this truth. Her life was not a single path, but many. She was a poet, a dancer, a singer, an activist, an author, and a storyteller. She was not one thing. She was transformation itself.

From an early age, she experienced trauma that left her silent. The world tried to shape her, to tell her who she was allowed to be. But silence did not break her—it led her to listen. To observe. To gather strength in stillness until her voice became undeniable.

The Art of Self-Reinvention

Redefining Identity – She did not remain within the labels given to her. She stepped beyond them, allowing herself to evolve, to shift, to become.

Owning Her Voice – Once silent, she became a poet whose words echoed across generations. She understood that true power does not come from the loudest voice but from the most authentic one.

Living Beyond Limitation – The world told her who she should be. She refused to be confined by those expectations. She lived, spoke, and created on her own terms.

Maya Angelou's life was not just a journey—it was a declaration: you are not bound by your past. You are not limited by what others believe is possible. You can begin again, and again, and again.

Key Points: Who you are is not a fixed story. Identity is not a prison—it is a choice. The moment you stop holding onto who you have been, you open the door to everything you can become.

❮❮ You are not here to be understood by everyone. You are here to be fully yourself. **❯❯**

The Book Jacket Exercise –
Writing the Summary of Who You Choose to Be

Every book has a cover. A title. A brief summary on the jacket, offering a glimpse of what lies within. The world sees this first—it shapes expectations, invites curiosity, and presents the essence of the story.

Your life, too, has a book jacket. But have you chosen what it says? Or has it been written for you?

The mind clings to identity, to the roles it has played, to the expectations it has accepted. *It says, This is who I am, and I cannot change.* But awareness reveals something deeper: who you are is not a fixed story. It is an unfolding, a presence beyond labels, beyond limitation.

You are not bound by the narratives of the past. You are not required to play the same role, to carry the same title, to live within the same description.

If you were to write the book jacket of your life—not as it has been, but as you choose it to be—what would it say?

Step 1: The Story You Are Ready to Tell

Imagine your life as a book. It has a cover. A title. A summary on the back, describing who you are and what this journey is about.

Now, write this summary not as a reflection of the past but as a declaration of presence.

Ask yourself:

> » *What is the essence of my story?*
>
> » *What qualities do I embody when I am fully present?*
>
> » *If I were not limited by old identities, how would I describe myself?*

Write a paragraph. Let it be simple and clear. Do not write what others expect. Write what is true.

Step 2: Seeing Beyond the Old Identity

Read what you wrote. Feel the words.

Now, ask yourself:

> » *Does this feel aligned with who I am, or is it shaped by who I have been?*

> » *Am I writing from fear or from presence?*

> » *If I released all doubt, all need for approval, would this still be my story?*

If any hesitation arises, simply observe it. It is not who you are—it is only a thought passing through awareness.

Step 3: Stepping Into It Fully

A book jacket is not just a summary. It is an invitation. It tells the world. This is what you will experience on *these pages*.

Now, ask yourself:

> » *If I were to live this story completely, how would I show up each day?*

> » *What choices align with this version of myself?*

> » *What would it feel like to embody this fully, without resistance?*

Let go of the old narrative. The one written for you. The one that no longer fits.

The world does not need the version of you that pleases others. It needs the version of you that is real, awake, and unguarded.

The story of who you are is not written in ink— it is written in awareness, moment by moment.

Exercise Reflection

The book jacket does not contain the whole story—it only introduces it.

And just as a book evolves with each chapter, so do you.

You are not a finished story. You are not a role to uphold. You are presence unfolding.

Who you choose to be is not a destination. It is this moment, now—lived fully, without hesitation.

• • •

The world doesn't need another imitation—it needs the real you. Your 'book jacket'—the way you present yourself— should match your true story. What is one step you can take today to align your external life with your inner truth?

We'd Love to Hear From You!

Thank you so much for reading this book-it means the world to me. If you found it helpful, inspiring, or just enjoyable, would you take a moment to leave a review? Your feedback not only helps others but also keeps me motivated to create more valuable content for you.

Here's how you can leave a review:

1. Scan the QR code on this page to go directly to the author's page.

2. Or, visit your Amazon Orders page, find this book, and click "Write a Product Review."

Your kind words make a big difference.
Thank you for your support!

The Ongoing Story of Self-Discovery

"There is no greater agony than bearing an untold story inside you."

— Maya Angelou

A book is never truly finished. The last page is only an invitation into what comes next.

Your life, too, is not a fixed story—it is unfolding, moment by moment. The mind may seek certainty, may try to define itself by past experiences, by what has been written before. But awareness reveals a deeper truth: who you are is not a story, but the presence in which all stories arise.

Self-Awareness and Transformation Are Continuous Edits

Growth is not something you achieve. It is something you allow.

The mind wants to hold onto identity—to say, *This is who I am, and this is how it must be.* But transformation does not happen in certainty. It happens in openness, in the willingness to see, to question, to shift.

You are not bound by old narratives. The past does not determine the next chapter unless you let it. Every moment is an opportunity to edit, to refine, to let go of what no longer aligns.

Who you were yesterday is not who you have to be today.

The Next Chapters Are Yours to Write

The mind may ask, *Where do I go from here? What is next?* But the future is not something to grasp. It is something that unfolds as you step into presence.

The next chapter is not waiting somewhere ahead. It is here, now, written in the choices you make in this moment.

Will you live from fear or from truth?

Will you continue the old script, or will you create something new?

Will you seek permission, or will you simply be?

The path is not something to find. It is something you walk, step by step, as you remain open to what is.

Final Reflections: Reading and Rewriting Your Life with Intention

You have been given many stories about who you are. Some were handed to you by others. Some were written by fear, by conditioning, by the mind's need for control.

But here is the truth: you are not the story. You are the awareness in which the story appears.

The mind may ask, *How do I rewrite my life?* But rewriting does not begin with force. It begins with seeing—seeing what is real, seeing what is illusion, seeing where you have been holding onto words that no longer serve you.

A book is not written all at once. Neither is transformation.

The only question is, what will you write next?

Let the old pages rest. Let presence guide the new.

Because your story is still unfolding.

• • •

Bibliography

Bandura, A. (1977). *Social learning theory*. Prentice-Hall.

Beck, A. T. (1979). *Cognitive therapy and the emotional disorders*. New York, NY: Penguin.

Bowlby, J. (1969). *Attachment and loss: Vol. 1. Attachment*. Basic Books.

Bronfenbrenner, U. (1979). *The ecology of human development: Experiments by nature and design*. Harvard University Press.

Bronfenbrenner, U. (1986). Ecology of the family as a context for human development: Research perspectives. *Developmental Psychology, 22*(6), 723–742.

Brown, B. (2012). *Daring greatly: How the courage to be vulnerable transforms the way we live, love, parent, and lead*. Avery.

Campbell, J. (1949). *The hero with a thousand faces*. Princeton, NJ: Princeton University Press.

Carrey, J. (2014). *Jim Carrey's Secret of Life Speech*. Maharishi International University. https://www.youtube.com/watch?v=V80-gPkpH6M

Csikszentmihalyi, M. (1990). *Flow: The psychology of optimal experience*. Harper & Row.

Dweck, C. S. (2006). *Mindset: The new psychology of success*. New York, NY: Random House.

Fanon, F. (1961). *The wretched of the Earth*. Grove Press.

Festinger, L. (1957). *A theory of cognitive dissonance*. Stanford University Press.

Frankl, V. E. (1984). *Man's search for meaning: An introduction to logotherapy*. Beacon Press.

Frankl, V. E. (2006). *Man's search for meaning* (Original work published 1946). Boston, MA: Beacon Press.

Gergen, K. J. (1991). *The saturated self: Dilemmas of identity in contemporary life*. New York, NY: Basic Books.

Gilbert, E. (2006). *Eat, pray, love: One woman's search for everything across Italy, India, and Indonesia*. New York, NY: Viking.

Gladwell, M. (2008). *Outliers: The story of success*. Little, Brown and Company.

Goleman, D. (1995). *Emotional intelligence: Why it can matter more than IQ*. Bantam Books.

James, W. (1890). *The principles of psychology*. Henry Holt and Co.

Jung, C. G. (1971). *Psychological types* (R. F. C. Hull, Trans.). Princeton University Press.

Kabat-Zinn, J. (1994). *Wherever you go, there you are: Mindfulness meditation in everyday life*. Hyperion.

Kahneman, D. (2011). *Thinking, fast and slow*. Farrar, Straus and Giroux.

Kotter, J. P. (1996). *Leading change*. Harvard Business Review Press.

Lewin, K. (1936). *Principles of topological psychology*. McGraw-Hill.

Lewis, C. S. (1952). *Mere Christianity*. New York, NY: HarperCollins.

Mbembe, A. (2001). *On the postcolony*. University of California Press.

McAdams, D. P. (1993). *The stories we live by: Personal myths and the making of the self.* The Guilford Press.

Mead, G. H. (1934). *Mind, self, and society*. University of Chicago Press.

Nisbett, R. E., & Cohen, D. (1996). *Culture of honor: The psychology of violence in the South*. Westview Press.

Noah, T. (2016). *Born a crime: Stories from a South African childhood*. Spiegel & Grau.

Prochaska, J. O., Norcross, J. C., & DiClemente, C. C. (1994). *Changing for good: A revolutionary six-stage program for overcoming bad habits and moving your life positively forward.* William Morrow.

Rogers, C. R. (1961). *On becoming a person: A therapist's view of psychotherapy*. Houghton Mifflin.

Schein, E. H. (2010). *Organizational culture and leadership*. Jossey-Bass.

Schwartz, J., & Gladding, R. (2011). *You are not your brain: The 4-step solution for changing bad habits, ending unhealthy thinking, and taking control of your life*. New York, NY: Avery.

Tolle, E. (1997). *The power of now: A guide to spiritual enlightenment*. Namaste Publishing.

Tolle, E. (1999). *The power of now: A guide to spiritual enlightenment*. New World Library.

Tolle, E. (2005). *A new earth: Awakening to your life's purpose*. New York, NY: Penguin Group.

Vygotsky, L. S. (1978). *Mind in society: The development of higher psychological processes*. Harvard University Press.